THE ENABI

Also by Roy McCloughry:

The Eye of the Needle
Taking Action
Men and Masculinity: From Power to Love
Aids: A Christian Response (with Carol Bebawi)
Ethical Tensions in the Welfare State
Belief in Politics
Men without Masks (with Roger Murphy)
Hearing Men's Voices
Population Growth and Christian Ethics
Debt (with Andrew Hartropp)
Living in the Presence of the Future
*Making a World of Difference: Christian Reflections
on Disability* (with Wayne Morris)
God, Sex, the Universe and All That

Edited by Roy McCloughry:
Issues Facing Christians Today (4th edition) by John Stott

THE ENABLED LIFE

Christianity in a disabling world

Roy McCloughry

First published in Great Britain in 2013

Society for Promoting Christian Knowledge
36 Causton Street
London SW1P 4ST
www.spckpublishing.co.uk

British Library Cataloguing-in-Publication Data
A catalogue record for this book is available from the British Library

ISBN 978−0−281−06278−2
eBook ISBN 978−0−281−07111−1

Typeset by Graphicraft Limited, Hong Kong
First printed in Great Britain by Ashford Colour Press
Subsequently digitally reprinted in Great Britain

eBook by Graphicraft Limited, Hong Kong

Produced on paper from sustainable forests

For my mother
Enid McCloughry
(1917–2013)
whose gentle Christian presence in my life
has been an inspiration

Contents

Acknowledgements

I still regard it as a privilege to be asked to put down some thoughts on paper with the assumption that others might want to read them. As someone involved in publishing I am aware of how many people are working industriously on books that will never see the light of day. What can be the justification for adding another book to groaning bookshelves everywhere?

I think there are subjects of such importance and urgency that it is an obligation to contribute something if one can. In my case this small book comes out of my own personal experiences and theological reflection on them. Although there are some ideas and passages that readers may find challenging, it is a book aimed at disabled people, their friends and colleagues as well as church and community leaders, and is written from a faith perspective. Those who want a more academic approach to the subject will find that authors such as Brian Brock, Deborah Creamer, Nancy Eiesland, Stanley Hauerwas, Hans Reinders, John Swinton, Amos Yong and Frances Young have written books that are illuminating and strategic in their approach to the subject. I have included a short guide to further reading at the end of this book.

I am grateful to the many people with whom I have had conversations over the years, including Brenda Darke, Christina Gangemi, Tim Hull, Lars Johansson, Jon Kuhrt, Nick Ladd, Alice Lawhead, Else Månsson, Helen McCloughry, Lizzie McCloughry, Joanna McCloughry, Lauren McCloughry, John Naudé, Ian Paul, Karin Ramachandra, Vinoth Ramachandra, Hans Reinders, Elisabeth Sandlund, Haydon Spenceley, John Swinton, Michele Taylor, Gordon Temple, Christopher Ward, Harriet Ward and

John Wyatt. None of the above should be construed as agreeing with anything in this book! I am particularly grateful to Haydon and to Gordon who read the manuscript and to Kate Ellis who transcribed the interview with Jean Vanier for me.

I am also grateful to successive years of students who have taken my lectures on personal and social ethics at St John's College, Nottingham and who have become interested in this subject. Most of them are, or will be, ministers in the Church of England and it is my hope that something of our time together will have affected their ministry for the good.

I am also grateful to Jean Vanier for being willing to see me at his home in Trosly-Breuil outside Paris in June 2012. Jean is now in his 80s and his kitchen table was piled high with books, manuscripts and tapes. He was very gracious in receiving Helen and myself when he was very busy. Seated opposite me and with eyes fixed on me as our conversation progressed, I was aware of a quality of listening that is rare. On occasions when talking of the gospel his face lit up with joy. Several times I was so moved that I found it difficult to carry on with the interview. Jean's life has been lived with people with profound intellectual impairments and he speaks as one who 'walks the talk'.

I would also like to thank those many people who have entrusted me with their stories, whether it was coming to see me following a talk in a church or a Christian festival such as Greenbelt, or more personally because they wanted to be heard by someone willing to listen to what had happened to them. In particular I would like to thank those who shared their stories with me on trips to Asia, Africa and Central America; they often seemed to be living in very challenging, or impossible, circumstances.

I am grateful to my friend, Alison Barr from SPCK, who edited an earlier book I wrote with Wayne Morris. She has been the epitome of patience and graciousness as the book refused to 'drop into her inbox'. Thank you, Alison. The trustees of the Kingdom Trust have been supportive of my work for many years and I am grateful to them as well. My thanks go to Martyn Eden, Peter Ellis, Richard Farnell, Jon Holt and Wendy Sayers.

My family and friends have been a great support. They are aware, more than any others, of the experiences out of which this book was born. They have witnessed the seizures, the side effects of drugs and the anxieties that go with living with someone with epilepsy. My thanks to them are incalculable. So to Joanna, Lizzie and Lauren, my wonderful daughters, who witnessed these things from a very young age, I am grateful for your love and support. I am grateful, in particular, to Lizzie who has allowed something of her own story to be included in this book. My sister Jean also lived with my condition, from the time I first had a convulsion as a baby when she was sent as a young child to get help.

My mother, who from my ninth year brought me up as a widowed single parent, enabled me to flourish by possessing that loving liberalism that appears to give a child freedom while maintaining invisible barriers around them. This book is dedicated to her, not just for that, but also for the fact that she has been an inspiration to me in my Christian life. Sadly for me but gloriously for her, she passed away while this book was in its last stages, at the age of 95. As I stood by her bedside in her last moments I signed her with the sign of the cross and read from 1 Corinthians 15.54–55: 'Death is swallowed up in victory. O death, where is your sting? O grave, where is your victory?' For me, that is an illustration of one of the themes of this book. What the world sees as weakness and defeat, the Christian sees as power and opportunity.

Finally, my thanks go to my wife Helen, who being lovely as she is could have got a better deal in a husband, but chose to bestow her love on this one. No man could wish for more.

Roy McCloughry
West Bridgford

A preliminary note

It is important to say something about language. Throughout the book I have used the term 'disabled people', which refers not only to people because they live with an impairment but also to the fact that they are disabled by social attitudes and other barriers. Often the word 'disabled' is seen as just applying to the body, for which I use the word 'impairment'. The question is, what complementary term should be used to describe people who do not have an impairment? Often the term 'able-bodied' is used, but this is not the complementary term to 'disabled' when it is used in this sense, as it refers only to the body and not to social attitudes and barriers. At other times the word 'non-disabled' is used, but this term defines people by a double negative which is not helpful. If we want to emphasize that disability is as much about inappropriate social attitudes and prejudices as it is about physical impairment, then the word to use is 'abled' rather than 'able-bodied'. What we need to show is how much of the identity of people who do not have an impairment is socially constructed. Some are *disabled* by society while others are *abled* by it. I want to highlight the extent to which those who do not have an impairment are privileged by the society that also disables those with an impairment.

However, I am as aware now as I have been over the last 15 years that you cannot win when it comes to the use of language, as it is so inextricably intertwined with ideology. I was grateful to commentators at the 2012 London Paralympics such as Dame Tanni Grey-Thompson, who went a long way to defusing this by drawing attention to the fact that the most important consideration is not wishing to cause offence rather than knowing the acceptable political language of the day.

I was not brought up to think of myself as a disabled person. Some would say that epilepsy is a 'disabling condition', making that a distinction. Epilepsy is one of those conditions where people affected can spend much of their time appearing to be healthy and functioning well, only to then experience a time when they are seriously debilitated by having a seizure. One can live in two worlds, and I discuss this in the book. For this reason readers will find that I sometimes include myself as a disabled person and at other times refer to disabled people more generally.

There is perhaps one other thing to say. In the West we are blessed with good medical care and a recently improved situation with respect to rights for disabled people although many disabled people live in poverty in this country. Many have also experienced heartache and injustice because of the current UK government's campaign to 'reassess' the suitability of disabled people to return to work. This seems to be based on the extraordinary idea that many disabled people are 'scroungers' and 'benefit cheats'. Although it has to be acknowledged that state benefits have to be adjusted from time to time, it has to be said that a nation should be judged by how it treats those who are poor and marginalized rather than how many 'freedoms' it creates for its wealthy. History may not judge this episode kindly.

However, while keeping this in mind I am also thinking of those in other parts of the world who are among the 650 million people who live with an impairment, or those who live with someone with an impairment. To walk the streets of Asia or Africa, or have the privilege of visiting people in their homes, is to become aware of the powerlessness and abject poverty in which many disabled people live in other parts of the world. They are frequently to be found among the poorest of the poor. I would ask readers of this book to have them in mind too – not just those of us who live in Western society.

1

Two worlds

A woman who is a wheelchair user is accustomed to others treating her as if she is only half there. People often talk over her head to the person pushing her wheelchair. Then one day she breaks her leg. She is still in her wheelchair but now has her leg very visibly in plaster. Everything changes. People now assume that she is a 'normal' person who has broken her leg and will be walking again soon. They treat her entirely differently. She is one of 'us'. They talk to her and treat her as a 'real' person. After a few weeks the plaster cast comes off and within days she returns to her previous experience of being overlooked. She is one of 'them'.

We live between two worlds. We see competition, ambition and autonomy as characteristic of the world of success. On the other hand we see disability, poverty and powerlessness as signs of a world haunted by endemic failure. We assume that the world of success has nothing to learn from the world of failure. It is best not to have anything to do with it. Of course, the media presents us with harrowing pictures of the 'other world', but we are well-practised voyeurs who do not engage easily. We are like tourists who have paid 'good money' to go on a guided tour of a shantytown but who are more concerned with taking photographs of people than relating to them. We may be money-rich but we are time-poor – we do not have the time to slow down and listen. We move on.

In a fast-moving world, 'making time' for someone is to give them significance in one's life. But there is a pressure in our culture to make time only for those things that benefit us.

In a competitive and ambitious world, we may see 'networking' as something that is beneficial but see ourselves as having too little time to spend on making friends. After all, true friendship is an end in itself, not a means to an end. To say of someone, 'I've got no time for her', is an act of judgement so complete that there is no comeback from its total rejection.

People who live in a world of success would like to seal it hermetically and deny that any other world exists. Yet from time to time they experience an irrational sense of fear. They know that there is just a thin veil separating being successful from being destitute, between successful relationships and being rejected, between being autonomous and being disabled. Elderly relatives may succumb to dementia, friends may be made redundant, people they love may die of cancer; and they are reminded that at any point they might find themselves living in a world they know little about and for which they are totally unprepared. They realize that they are only *temporarily* abled.

These two worlds, far from running in parallel, are closely intertwined. To befriend people who have experienced brokenness is to realize that although at that point their story may differ from ours, they are no different from us. We become more human as we learn from one another, and to do so is to make time for one another. It is time rather than money that ends up bestowing the greater affirmation upon another person. In a universe of two worlds where one is characterized by success and the other by apparent failure, all cross-cultural relationships are asymmetric. Friendship is impossible because the world of success cannot admit that it can learn from the world of failure, and the world of failure can find no place in the world of success.

If I believe that who I am depends on what I have achieved, I am unlikely to value the life of someone with an intellectual impairment. I can live my life without that person. To break this deadlock takes courage. It can only be done by realizing that there is no 'us' and 'them' – there has only ever been 'us'. We are not doing things 'to' other people, nor are we doing things 'for' other people. We can only do things 'with' other people. People like us.

It takes a revolution in thinking for a person rushing through the day aided by the accoutrements of time-saving tablet PCs, computers and mobile phones to realize that the wheelchair user they have just ignored, who they pass every day, might be the one who can rescue them from the dehumanizing fate that is rapidly approaching. To be successful in a world so distorted that it drives people to prefer the material to the spiritual and status to friendship is to trade one's soul for the ephemeral. The fact is that in order to change a society in which disabled people are excluded, I have to change *my* life. This is the task of theological reflection, discussed later in this book. It is not something that is addressed by the disability rights literature, which, like politics in general, talks the language of justice but not the language of love.

We are most ourselves when we are present with one another. Being able to do this requires a degree of stillness and a willingness to see being with another person as worthwhile, when previously we might have viewed it as wasting time. Nor are we most human when we are receiving something worthwhile from another person. Love does not require reciprocity. A friend does not have to speak or be coherent. Listening conveys love. True friendship is based not on what I receive from other people but on loving them for their own sake. Jean Vanier talks about this in the conversation at the end of this book.

But in a world where some are too busy to be attentive to other people, and where in turn others have been led to believe that they are unworthy of those attentions, love is rarely to be found. Of course, decent people can act in a friendly way towards another person, but to involve oneself in friendship is quite another matter.

When we reflect on the world of disability and the challenges and opportunities it represents, the question we face is, 'How can we bring these two worlds together so that we can learn together what it means to be human?' It is impossible to develop any kind of Christian perspective on disability without the two worlds coming together. The problem is that there are major hazards in both worlds that prevent us closing the gap. These may be invisible to us: often our most powerful beliefs are the ones we are least aware of. Those of us who are prejudiced against disabled people may well protest the loudest when we are accused. Self-delusion is everywhere and we have the capacity to pull the wool over our own eyes. When we befriend someone who is very different from us, they may begin to tell us that they see us differently from the way we see ourselves. In complete contrast, spending time in the company of people who have identical views and backgrounds to ourselves means that we are rarely challenged and will never learn to see the world differently. It is when we open up to those who are different from ourselves that we begin to grow as human beings.

The problem that arises between abled and disabled people is one of power. People who are abled and hold positions of power make many of the decisions that affect disabled people. Politicians and policymakers rarely see the world through the eyes of disabled people, even when they are appointed to committees to advise them. Disabled people have to live in a world made by and for abled people. The onus is on disabled people to raise awareness that they have additional needs that have not been taken into account or perspectives that have not been appreciated. It is true that legislation in recent years has attempted to bring about equality in this area, but in every part of life there are still huge barriers to be overcome. It is ironic that it is those who may feel most powerless who constantly have to take the initiative to remind society of their presence. The invisibility of disabled people in the community and in public debate leads to their additional needs being overlooked.

Such invisibility can lead to disabled people being stereotyped only as consumers of community resources rather than also being contributors to its culture.

The fact that power belongs to abled people means that a friendship between abled and disabled people has to start by disabled people becoming visible. In societies where disabled people are hidden (sometimes literally) from the community, no such friendship can occur. As one writer has put it, 'to belong I need to be missed'.[1]

There has been much talk recently about the idea of 'inclusion' in the disability context. An inclusive community is one where abled and disabled people are present on equal terms. They have the possibility of interacting and forming relationships. Yet there are two issues here that need to be confronted. First, it is often the case that in order for disabled people to be in a position to access such a community there needs to be positive discrimination. Just in terms of attending a meeting: they may need the provision of transport in order to find their way there, or a venue that provides the facilities they need during the evening. Second, being an inclusive community is still based on abled people 'including' disabled people. It is abled people who do the including, not disabled people. They are the objects of inclusion. Under inclusion, power can still belong to the abled person. There are a thousand reasons why abled people may not wish to belong to such an inclusive community, because they do not see forming a relationship with a disabled person as being worth the effort.

Despite this, inclusion is vital if disabled people are to exercise power. This will never happen unless they are enabled to participate in such a community. Participation is an active word, not a passive one. The virtue of inclusion is, however, that it highlights the barriers that prevent disabled people participating in the community. The Paralympics in 2012 were a success because the concept and practice of inclusion was central to all that went on. But the most visible aspect of the games was that they were about participation. The sporting venues were packed with spectators who wanted to support disabled athletes' participation in their chosen sport, and who wanted them to excel at it. Inclusion is the foundation on which participation is built.

Of course, the use of the word 'inclusive' has developed as we have discovered how 'exclusive' contemporary society is of disabled people. The kind of community we want to see is helped rather than hindered by such an insight. But the politics of inclusion must be egalitarian, active and participatory. If people are disabled by the barriers others place in front of them, they will never be able to celebrate their potential.

2

A story and a meditation

Recent books on disability and Christianity have often included descriptions of the author's own experience of disability (although hopefully we are past the days when an author on the subject had no credibility without a personal experience of disability). We now recognize that many people whose lives are touched by disability have important insights to share even though they do not live with an impairment themselves. Nevertheless, I am aware that personal experience fundamentally affects the way a person sees the world. It also affects the way in which they are perceived by the world.

My own story is about living with epilepsy. About 50 million people in the world live with some kind of epilepsy; 80 per cent of them are in developing regions of the world.[1] About 75 per cent of people with the condition in these regions do not get the treatment they need (epilepsy responds to treatment in about 70 per cent of cases). In Africa around nine out of ten people with epilepsy go untreated. Death rates are two to three times higher in people with epilepsy than in the general population. Risk of sudden death is 24 times greater.

Even in the UK there is a real shortage of doctors, nurses and therapists who specialize in epilepsy, despite the fact that around 600,000 people have epilepsy. Only 52 per cent of people with epilepsy in the UK are seizure-free, although it is estimated that the figure could rise to 70 per cent if they had the right treatment.[2] Despite the Equalities Act 2010 and other legislation requiring that people with epilepsy have equal access to employment, education and other necessary resources,

I have heard story after story from people with epilepsy telling of rejection, discrimination and exclusion, as well as an inability to access the services they need. Worldwide, epilepsy is a condition that is still accompanied by massive stigma and discrimination.

- In both China and India, epilepsy is commonly viewed as a reason for prohibiting or annulling marriages.
- In the United Kingdom, a law forbidding people with epilepsy to marry was repealed only in 1970.
- In the United States, until the 1970s it was legal to deny people with seizures access to restaurants, theatres, recreational centres and other public buildings.

I have lived with epilepsy all my life. There are other conditions I live with, such as Type 1 diabetes and moderate but progressive hearing loss, but it is my experience of epilepsy that has had the most profound impact on my life. It is important to say a little about how it has affected me because living with epilepsy changed my view of myself and my view of God.

It started in infancy with what were then called 'absences', where I would drift off and not respond to any stimuli. Occasionally I would fall, or get myself into a position where if I had not been found I could have suffocated. Between the ages of 9 and 14 I was relatively free from seizures of any sort, but when I was 14 I had a major seizure at a party. It was my introduction to the premier league of tonic-clonic seizures which, by all accounts, can be pretty upsetting to watch. (There are around 40 different kinds of epilepsy.) I had gone to the party keen to meet a girl, but when I came round, confused, I fancied that the seizure would not have enamoured me to her.

With epilepsy (as with many other conditions) you lose control of your own story. Being in control of your own story is highly prized in our society; indeed, it is essential if you want to be seen as an achiever. We probably all fear the ways in which we might lose that control, such as homelessness, imprisonment, redundancy or bankruptcy – experiences in which we might lose identity and a sense of self, and feel diminished as human beings as a result.

Being in control is valued because it is an expression of power. Lack of control is seen as weakness or alternatively that you are a danger to others as you are 'out of control'. There is a sense of helplessness about having a seizure: you realize that soon you will be unconscious but you are about to provide a memorable(!) episode in the story of those with you at the time. You have never witnessed your own seizures, while others have. Epilepsy can undermine security of identity. You realize that others know things about you that are unknown to you, and this can introduce an uncertainty in you about who you are and whether you are acceptable to others any more. Will the girl you were fond of at the party ever want to speak to you again? You are no longer sure. Uncertainty can erode identity, and people with epilepsy often find it difficult to mix or hold their own socially.

Epilepsy is a hidden but disabling condition. In many instances it is well controlled by medication – although some people can have dozens of seizures a day, and others may experience severe side effects from powerful anti-epileptic drugs (AEDs). It may be that nobody even knows that you live with the condition, if it is effectively controlled by drugs, or if the kind of epilepsy you have is not accompanied by loss of consciousness, or only affects you at night.

But if you have a 'full-blown' seizure those around you might well be shocked. You come round, hardly able to walk and with a 'breeze-blocker' of a headache. You are aware that you have had a seizure but cannot usually remember what happened. Your brain is scrambled. Others may not want to give you the whole picture, perhaps wishing to spare you the details. You may find yourself in a hospital A & E department, with a clipboard resting on your stomach (you are still on an ambulance trolley) that bears the words 'known epileptic' – a description that I feel does not do justice to my personality. You might be there for several hours, during which time you will mull over the fact that you will have to hand your driving licence in again and wait for another year before you can drive. (It used to be three years.)[3] That means that your wife will have to do the driving when you go away on holiday or any appreciable distance – something that seems unfair. You will also have time to anticipate that your drug prescription may have to be adjusted yet again, and that might cause more seizures in the transitional stage and side effects from the new drugs. You may feel guilty because you forgot to take your medication that morning, partly, ironically, because you have a poor memory due to years of living with epilepsy and powerful AEDs. It's a lot to think about while shivering on a hospital trolley because your body is still suffering from shock.

I have been interested in my own attempts to minimize the embarrassment I feel at having a seizure. They are irrational, while remaining entirely understandable. When I become aware that I am about to have a seizure I know that I am going to fall to the ground and possibly injure myself. The rational thing to do in the short amount of time I might have before the seizure is to lie down where I am. Yet I have never done so. This is certainly a painful application of the saying, 'Pride comes before a fall'!

On a few occasions I have carried on for some time knowing I am going to have a seizure. I once walked through Nottingham looking for the best place to keel over. I remember going past a branch of the fashion designer Paul Smith. I spared the elegant young men posing in the shop and voted instead to grace the public library with my – soon to be memorable – presence. For some reason the public sector seems to provide a psychological haven. Inexplicably, I got the lift to the business section on the first floor, went over to the librarian and simply said, 'I don't feel very well.' Given that the library is a monument to the transmission of information I can safely say, with hindsight, that this remark did not describe what was about to happen in its entirety. She said, 'I'll get you a glass of water', which was understandable, but since that too would shortly be on the carpet her response was more than a little short of adequate, although not her fault. The next thing I knew, I was in the back of an ambulance with my wife, who had been called out of a meeting and was looking frustrated as an ambulance wasn't necessary. This was another thing that the librarian was not to know. Sitting somewhere safe until I recovered would have been enough.

It is perhaps useful to explain that before I have a seizure I have what is called an 'aura'. People with epilepsy differ in their experiences: it depends where in the brain the seizure originates. Some have seizures without any warning that they are going to happen. Some people notice a smell or a noise. My own warning signs come in several stages. The aura is the one thing in my life that induces fear in me, as although I don't experience the seizure, I am aware of the aura.

People with epilepsy, even if they have been taking drugs for years to control the condition (as I have), will constantly monitor the inside of their head for a sign that something may be wrong. Think of it as sonar, looking out for a blip on the screen that might signify the presence of another vessel (in this case, hostile). In my own experience I develop a deep sense of confusion, which ends in the seizure. Imagine your mind as a calm sea. You are in a small boat enjoying the day. All is well with the world. Then you become aware of the smallest ripple passing under the boat. Instantly you are alert. A person who has no neurological condition would not even notice it, but you are now waiting for further movement. You begin to look at how far you are away from the land and safety in case things escalate fast. Of course, the small ripple might not develop into anything bigger but you have an increasing sense of both uncertainty and anxiety. Then a second wave comes, this time higher and faster. This is followed by a third and a fourth until you are experiencing a 'brainstorm'.[4] The boat is being tossed around until it capsizes and you are thrown into the water and lose consciousness.

What are these 'waves' that lead to a seizure? For me they are different kinds of confusion. It might help to divide them into stages even if doing so is a little artificial. My mind splits into two. One part focuses on thinking about what to do practically – where nearby would be best to have a seizure – and the other tries to focus on something despite the confusion (usually counting to a hundred). Yet the rational aspect of my brain is gradually being taken over by a process over which I have no control. This can take minutes or seconds, during which time I have an overwhelming sense of confusion that can include powerful experiences of déjà vu. It is this process that is terrifying and so foreign to any normal sense of control. It is the brewing of a storm on water, and is as real as that. So what are the stages?

- Not knowing where I am: I don't recognize anywhere, even in my own house.
- Not knowing who you are: you are becoming an object, not a human being.
- Not knowing who I am: I am no longer thinking of myself as a person – Roy.
- Not knowing what my body is: hands or feet mean nothing.
- Not knowing how to speak.
- Not knowing where I am in space: up, down, floating, standing merges.

This sense of disorientation ends when the muscles in my body contract. My head is pulled round to the right and the muscles in my chest contract, pushing out the air in my lungs over my voice box so that I appear to shout loudly.

My daughter, now 29, had uncontrolled epilepsy until she was 24, when she had neurosurgery. Surgeons cut out part of the hippocampus in the centre of her brain and she has been well since then, although she still takes one AED as a precautionary measure. I remember sitting round the dinner table as a family sometimes having our own version of the old show *This is Your Life*, called 'Fits we have known'. These have included some terrifying experiences, but there were, with hindsight, some very funny episodes. I once went to preach at a well-known church in the West End of London. As I walked into the vestibule I saw a 'man of the road' having a cup of tea, looking the worse for wear. On my way to the church I had become aware that an aura was developing, but as usual hoped it would just disappear. Doggedly, I carried on, and at the point where the curate was welcoming me as the guest preacher I dropped like a stone. I came round to find the homeless man staring at me as if he thought his life wasn't so bad after all. I also was aware of the curate looking at me not with compassion but with the terror of a man who may have to give a sermon at a moment's notice. I insisted on preaching – it was a rather garbled message – holding myself up by gripping the pulpit. I wasn't invited back. Fair enough. As I was speaking even I knew that I was making about as much sense as a monkey who had drunk one too many vodkas. I was preaching before an elegantly attired and coiffured Kensington congregation, while I was dressed in borrowed clothes that appeared to include the Rector's gardening trousers.

Lizzie, my daughter, who used to become very confused, once left a bus shouting to everybody, 'I love you all!' But another time she was brought home by a kindly taxi driver who had found her disorientated in the street. Friends have had to rescue her from wandering off when they were out together in the evening. On one occasion she was picked up by the police and she sat in the back of a police car trying to explain that she wasn't drunk but had epilepsy. At home we would sometimes hear a crash from upstairs because she had fallen. In work she found people's attitudes unhelpful even when she had a job with the health service! As an attractive and vivacious teenager she had some loyal friends, but few teenagers will befriend someone who is prone to keeling over with no notice or begins to say strange things.

I was advised, as a young man, not to apply for training as a priest in the Church of England as it would not ordain an 'epileptic', but I have since spoken from hundreds of Church of England pulpits. I was turned down for a place at an Oxbridge college because, as I was told at interview, the stress would be too much for me, 'as an epileptic'.[5] Sadly, discrimination has not disappeared in the intervening years, despite changes in the law. As my daughter Lizzie has found in the world of work, people can discriminate in many ways, perhaps trying to ease you out of their organization citing some spurious reason. Fortunately, she is excellent at what she does and this has been rewarded with a great job and a supportive manager.

Living with mystery

Despite the fact that we know so much about the workings of the brain and have access to MRI scans and EEGs, there is still a mystery associated with epilepsy as well as myth and stigma. Perhaps the Bible is partly to blame. Certainly as a young man I was confused by the fact that Jesus seemed to accept the contemporary view that someone who experienced seizures was demon-possessed. One translation of the Bible (New Revised Standard Version) even goes so far as to call the demon-possessed boy an epileptic (Matthew 17.14–20). What are the options in interpreting the biblical text?

- Jesus was wrong. The boy just had epilepsy. Jesus was subject to the degree of medical knowledge that was prevalent in his day. He went along with the diagnosis of the boy's father. Yet we are told that a demon was present and that when he had cast it out the boy was restored to health.

- Jesus was right. The boy was demon-possessed, and this presented as if he had epilepsy but in fact he did not. Jesus acted appropriately. Therefore the NRSV translation is spurious and offensive.
- Jesus was right but the conclusion is that all people with epilepsy are demon-possessed.

Obviously I am not going to opt for the last option, and I favour the second. All this assumes that I want to take the Bible seriously, as I view it as the authoritative basis for the Christian faith. If I were not bound by that discipline then I could dismiss such a passage because it does not suit me or it is not in accordance with modern beliefs.

Many thousands of people around the world who live in traditional cultures are still thought of as being preyed upon by evil spirits. Misunderstandings about epilepsy from around the world continue to be prevalent in the twenty-first century.[6]

- In Cameroon it is believed that people with epilepsy are inhabited by the devil. They are not seen as evil, but the belief is that evil invades them and causes them to convulse from time to time.
- In some rural areas of India, attempts are made to exorcise evil spirits from people with epilepsy – by tying them to trees, beating them, cutting a portion of hair from their head, squeezing lemon and other juices over their head and starving them.
- In Indonesia epilepsy is often considered to be a punishment from unknown dark forces.
- In Liberia the cause of epilepsy is perceived as related to witchcraft or evil spirits.
- In Nepal epilepsy is associated with weakness, possession by an evil spirit or the reflection of a red colour. Bystanders who witness a seizure will often spray water on the forehead of the person experiencing the seizure, or make him or her smell a leather shoe.

- In the Netherlands in 1996, a person was allegedly whipped and put into isolation because her seizures were thought to result from magic.
- In Swaziland many traditional healers mention sorcery as the cause of epilepsy.
- In Uganda, as in many other countries, epilepsy is thought to be contagious, and so people with epilepsy are not allowed to eat from the communal food pot for fear of others contracting it through that person's saliva.

Also, in many parts of Asia the idea of 'karma' is very important. That is, your experience and status in this life reflects things you have done in a previous life. If you suffer in some way or are disabled, this might mean that you did something wrong in your previous life. I became acutely aware of this recently on a visit to Asia, when I talked to parents of disabled children; they told me that it was difficult to access services or to get people to listen to their problems, as the prevalent attitude was, 'You or your child must have done something terribly wrong to deserve this.' Although Christianity does not accept the concept of karma, it was present in the society of Jesus' day, as in the case of the man born blind (John 9.1–41).

In terms of the boy who was demon-possessed, we are left with a set of options, all of which leave me uneasy for different reasons. First, in the modern world we are not familiar with the idea of demon possession. We believe in the power of reason and in the ability of science to explain phenomena that formerly were explained by the presence of the supernatural. So we could say that since no one knew about epilepsy or the workings of the brain in Jesus' day, the fact that a person was 'out of control' meant that they had been 'taken over', and since what was happening appeared 'evil' the blame could only be laid at the door of the presence of evil spirits.

Second, the Gospel writers repeatedly describe Jesus as casting out demons. This problem relates to the truthfulness of the accounts. What did they see? Why did they describe this as demonic if it was not? Jesus certainly believed that he had cast out a demon, and he did this countless times. It was a familiar part of his ministry. If we believe that these accounts never happened or were exaggerated, what can we believe about Scripture?

We need to be extremely cautious about coming to the conclusion that someone is demon-possessed today, having witnessed the suffering that such a label can bring. But those who believe in the presence of the supernatural in contemporary life will never want to rule it out. In the New Testament passages, if these people were demon-possessed, as it seems they were, then some of them presented as if they were people with epilepsy. The reverse is not true – people with epilepsy are not demon-possessed. Epilepsy has no deep meaning. It is simply what happens when the brain gets out of sync. There is no more need to look for supernatural causes than we would for any other impairment. The juxtaposition of these two things throughout history has led to great suffering and stigmatization for people with epilepsy everywhere.

Living with the consequences

The consequences of living with epilepsy are many, but they are not all bad. My life is a mixture of the strong and the vulnerable, the capable and the uncontrollable, the ordinary and the extraordinary, the routine and the dangerous, the joyful and the banal. For me the modern idea of being autonomous, of not needing other people, is not an option. I need the people who make the drugs that keep me functioning. I need the kindness of strangers in the street. I need friends who will not think less of me after they have witnessed a seizure. I want to live in a world that is defined by the quality of its relationships rather than its ability to create wealth, and in which people admit they are vulnerable, rather than pretend they are always strong. Epilepsy is not some curse from God or a sign that I have sinned or lack the faith to be healed. It is instead a 'strange gift' from God.

First, my whole life is a gift from God. That does not refer just to those elements that I regard as a blessing, but also to the struggles, the pain and the failure. Otherwise my life would be reduced to an amateur's doodle rather than the masterpiece in oils that is the life of every human being. When life turns to ashes in our mouths we cannot pretend that God is not involved, or, embarrassed, lock him away in a cupboard until the good times return and with them our pride in the goodness of God. Faith is willing to believe in the goodness of God even when the evidence suggests otherwise. It doesn't require us to put on a false smile and pretend everything is OK. But it does mean that in whatever we are going through there is a thread of hope – even if we cannot believe that for ourselves and others have to believe it for us.

Second, my life is a gift to the world. If I did not live with epilepsy I would not be the slightest bit interested in disability or in talking to disabled people. And sadly, that's true of the majority of people, inside and outside the Church. For instance, compare the numbers of people you would expect to turn up to a talk on disability with those for a talk on healing. Disability is not a popular subject. 'Are you sure you want to get involved in disability issues?' a friend asked me. 'Your profile will sink, invitations to speak will dry up.' But as I told him, I have no option. I have been given this experience to use, as with every other element of my life. It is my gift to the world. A strange one, but a gift nevertheless.

Of course, this is my personal interpretation of the situation, and each of us has questions about our lives and their significance, whether we are disabled people or not. I would not want others with an impairment to feel under pressure to say that their condition is a 'gift from God' if they feel that it is God who is currently destroying their lives. What is important is that as a community we reflect together on the significance of our lives. One of the most disabling activities in life happens when others debate the meaning of your life without consulting you about it. Yet this is repeatedly done to disabled people.

An interesting aspect of God's relationship to us comes out of the incident when Moses stands before the burning bush and God tells him to go to Pharaoh to ask for the liberation of his people. Moses makes several excuses. One of them is that he has a speech defect, which is why in the end God sends Aaron to go with him. But God also says something else: 'The LORD said to him, "Who gave human beings their mouths? Who makes them deaf or mute? Who gives them sight or makes them blind? Is it not I, the LORD?"' (Exod. 4.11).

God is the creator of everyone, and does not distinguish between people because of their body shape or their impairment. We are equal before him. He is not surprised that some people are born with an impairment, nor are they any less useful to him. After all, many key figures in the Bible had an impairment. This is not God stating that people with an impairment have been judged by him. Quite the opposite. This is the Creator speaking of his commitment to all of his creation. God sees us. God owns us as his. God uses us, as he did Moses. Disabled people are no different from anyone else in their calling before God. They have questions and answers, strengths and weaknesses, unique perspectives and common experiences, as do the rest of the population.

Disabled people want to make sense of their lives just as much as everyone else does. A story is told about a theologian who had a special interest in disability. He had no impairment and knew few, if any, disabled people. He was invited to give a paper on 'suffering' to an invited academic audience. The evening went well. He was listened to politely, applauded and the question time consisted of a series of carefully articulated academic points. He was pleased with the evening and thought at the end that he might even publish what he had said. Then another group invited him to speak, to give the same talk. He had not heard of them but was so buoyed up by his recent success that he accepted. As he walked on to the stage he found himself faced with an audience composed entirely of severely disabled people. They were eager to hear what he had to say on the subject. The question of 'suffering' was one that they had faced in their own minds hundreds of times. But the theologian stood on the stage and realized that he had nothing to say to these people.

Things could have been so different. It is not that academic thinking is not valuable – after all, the question of suffering is a deeply philosophical one. But it had not occurred to the theologian to develop his reflections alongside disabled people, learning from them and debating with them. He had not thought of it as a biographical question. He made his excuses and left the stage, leaving the audience disappointed and confused.

Making sense of our lives is a community undertaking. We are 'people in relationship' and we need to know and be known by others if we are to find meaning for our existence and, indeed, to understand what God is doing in our lives.

Some time ago I was asked to write a prayer or meditation on the theme of 'work'. This was my offering.

A meditation: on having a fit at work[7]

Sitting at the boardroom table
I idly bask in the sunshine pouring through the window.
Then as I yawn and glance at my watch,
bells and whistles go off in my head.
I am instantly alert
as if a bucket of cold water has been
    thrown over me.
The others doze on –
can they tell?
They'll know soon enough.

How long do I have?
A minute?
The first wave of confusion arrives,
rolling over the surface of my brain
   like a ripple on treacle.
Where will I fall?
Not on Suzy, please, God.
Not on the boss;
though those thighs would amply break my fall.

Please, not an ambulance,
I don't want to be wheeled incontinent
through Accounts
only to wait on a trolley down the local
until my exhausted legs can bear my weight
and the pain in my scrambled head retreats.

Have I got time to leave the room,
To make it look like 'a comfort break'?
No. The door opens.
I enter the world of the surreal,
staggering drunkenly through the valley
of shadows
as the world drains of meaning.
I become afraid: very afraid.

I no longer know who I am
or where I am
or who they are
or where the floor is
or what a floor is
wave follows wave of confusion.

I hear someone cry out.
Heads turn.
I fall.
Forget the legislation
There goes the promotion.

3

Disability in perspective

How are we to understand disability? In some cases we tend to sum up the situation just by looking at a person in the wheelchair, noticing the hearing aids in a person's ears or seeing someone walking along the street scanning the ground with a cane because he or she is visually impaired. We think we know what these words mean, and often do not care to ask others what the words mean for them. We prefer to fit disabled people into our world rather than enter their world and ask them what life looks like from their perspective. I can count on the fingers of one hand the number of people who have asked me what it is like to have epilepsy. People would rather live with their own self-constructed ideas.

To base our understanding of disability on what we see is as mistaken as claiming to understand women by looking at their bodies. It treats the person as an object to be described rather than as a person with whom to have a relationship. Yet so many people cannot get past this. They have a fear of the impairment itself, which is irrational. They cannot see that they are the ones with the problem. If you had an irrational fear of people of the opposite sex, or from a different ethnic group, then without hesitation you would be advised to seek help. Yet negative attitudes towards disabled people are so pervasive that they have become invisible to us.

We all live with assumptions about life that we take for granted. They may have been a part of our family upbringing or education. Perhaps we have had experiences that have shaped our view of the world or have been influenced by particular leaders in our formative years. These assumptions may be so much a part of us that we cannot see them or evaluate them. When we do express them we see them as 'common sense' or as natural, neutral and normal. They have become invisible to us. As the Chinese proverb has it, 'A fish discovers water last'. It is not aware of the water because it has always been in it. If we hold views that although unfair are generally accepted throughout society, then those holding such views will continue to live without being challenged. It is left to the minority, the excluded, to protest.

Over the last century we have seen successive protest movements against dominant ideologies that saw themselves as benign but were guilty of injustice and prejudice of extraordinary proportions. The fight against racism will go on for many decades but was started by brave people who took on the status quo. Women dared to make a stand against patriarchy, and in showing that they thought differently from men they made distorted masculinities visible to men to whom those attitudes were as natural as the air they breathed.

Another way of talking about the power of the invisible is to look at what we call 'normal'. We do not see those things that we regard as 'normal' as being, by definition, 'out of the ordinary'. They are, quite literally, the 'norm' – the standard by which we judge everything else. Therefore we do not have to deal with the normal until we come across something that does not fit into that category. Only then do we need to decide what to do with it. Do we have a negative or positive attitude to it? Should we celebrate or deride it? People who live 'normal' lives do not have to think about them. They may have enough money, health and power to be comfortable and to surround themselves with like-minded people. They are not going to be the ones who will challenge the prevailing culture or prophesy against it. They have too much to lose.

Of all the invisible powers that govern our lives, none is greater than the power of 'normality'. Those who live according to the normal confer on it a moral status. To be normal is 'good'. What are the alternatives? To be 'subnormal' or 'abnormal'? Neither of these descriptions should be applied to any human being.

Yet 'normal' is not necessarily *morally* good. To use it in that way gives it a false power. There are other words that have achieved this pseudo-moral status. Words that fall into the same category include 'progress'. To make progress is seen to be a 'good thing'. How about the word 'need'? Meeting need is seen to be a good thing. But none of these words by themselves have a moral status. For that to happen we have to decide what we are progressing *towards*, what the need is that should be met, and what it is that we regard as normal. It is only recently, for instance, that we have come to question previously held beliefs about economic progress because of the impact of those beliefs on climate change and on the way in which one generation borrowed from another in order to finance an unsustainable boom. In the same way, just saying that something is 'normal' is not enough to conclude that it is good. Our assumptions about what is normal have so much power in our lives that we can talk quite literally about the 'tyranny of normality'. Indeed, some writers now talk of 'normalcy' as a world-view.

This has enormous implications when it comes to thinking about disability. The negative connotations, stereotypes and prejudices associated with disability show that to be disabled is to be considered outside the sphere of the normal. Changing that attitude is a daunting task, and has been for many decades. Other movements, such as women's rights and anti-racism, have demonstrated that challenging unjust structures is painstaking work that advances slowly most of the time.

Approaching disability from this perspective shows that we are looking at far more than the nature of the body. Disability is also to do with the attitudes and actions that disable people. A physical or intellectual impairment may mean that someone cannot perform certain functions. But that person might say that 'disabled' is not a noun or an adjective that describes them as an individual, but a verb that describes actions and attitudes towards them. They live, as the subtitle of this book indicates, in a 'disabling world'.

The medical model

Two models are frequently used when talking about disability issues, the first being the medical model and the second the social model. Neither is adequate from a Christian perspective. Both are *necessary* but not *sufficient*. As a person living with epilepsy I need both insights. I live in both worlds.

The medical model focuses on the body and its impairments. I may go to the neurology clinic to undergo tests for epilepsy or to have my drugs and toxicity levels reassessed. I depend on the fact that my neurologist is well trained, understands what he is doing and respects me enough to explain to me what is going on. I see our relationship as a partnership where I can provide some of the information that he needs and vice versa. (In fact in these days of the internet I may have a surfeit of information on my condition!) It is worth saying, however, that through my experience of epilepsy I know that he will probably also see people with severe epilepsy who do not understand much about what is going on and are entirely in his hands. In those situations he is looking to family and friends to support and represent the interests of these vulnerable adults.

All this is about my impairment, strictly defined. Yet we know from research that people with epilepsy often do not like going to hospital clinics or having tests. Some decide not to keep their appointments; others may have memory problems and just forget about them. People with epilepsy have a high likelihood of being unemployed; they may have lifestyles that are disorganized or chaotic. Still others live with depression or other mental health issues. It is a disabling condition and has consequences that reach far outside the hospital consulting room.

For this reason even the most able doctors need to see themselves as part of a team. The future of the medical model is as a contribution to integration in which medical expertise is brought together with the experience of social services, social workers, counsellors, people living with the condition, local community leaders and others, with the aim of obtaining a full picture of the affected individuals' needs and how they can be enabled to self-manage their lives, and indeed to flourish rather than just survive.

The need for a mixture of expertise, humility and partnership is a powerful one, but if the protests of the disability movement are anything to go by, it is frequently not evident in the interaction between disabled people and the medical profession. In fact many disabled people point to the attitudes of the medical profession as disabling rather than enabling. The very expertise that enables a doctor to focus on the minutiae of a condition may distance her from the person with that condition.

Certain disability activists want to reject the idea that disability has anything to do with dysfunction, in order to rid the concept of disability of any remotely negative association, seeing it rather as a form of cultural diversity. This view of disability as diversity is important as it lifts disability out of the negative confines into which it is often trapped. But I for one cannot pretend that my brain is completely functional. What does matter is that my personal identity is not defined by that dysfunction. What happens, though, is that the closer I get to the hospital environment the more I am aware that for some people in that environment, all they know about me is contained in my medical notes. I feel defined by my medical condition. The acute hospital is part of a 'culture of cure' that often feels uncomfortable for the person with a long-term condition.

But at times, of course, the 'culture of cure' works well. To be fair, when my daughter had neurosurgery I did not care

27

greatly about having a warm personal relationship with the surgeon. What I wanted to know was how many times he had performed the procedure and what his success rate was. The fact that we had the full attention of a large team of experts over several years who were deeply compassionate and interested in her was a welcome surprise. It made things much easier for her to be treated as a human being, so that her questions were answered honestly and clearly, and she felt that she mattered. It has always seemed to me that we must applaud best practice wherever we find it, even (or perhaps especially) when it doesn't sit easily with our ideological commitments.

But I am aware that the millimetre that is explored in the hospital is often unrelated to the kilometre that is the rest of a person's life. People do not want major decisions affecting them to be declared from Mount Olympus by the medical expert, or indeed any expert. These days, authority cannot be assumed; it has to be earned. People wish to be consulted, and to make decisions jointly with all those involved. It needs to be a genuine partnership. The doctor may have seen cases such as ours hundreds of times, and knows what her treatment plan is. But everyone is unique and needs to be heard; we should be spoken to in a language we can understand and asked for our opinion. The doctor may make the diagnosis, but it is our story and our life. This is also a part of the respect we owe each other.

The problems associated with my condition cannot be addressed by a medical specialist alone, which is why integration with other perspectives is necessary and community-based medicine, where people work in teams, is the way forward. The stigma and discrimination associated with epilepsy are present throughout society; it needs more than a medical consultation to overcome them. Yet the medical profession could do a great deal in combating those negative social forces if they were more open to becoming partners with others in campaigning for change.

Focusing on the body is necessary but not sufficient. The disability movement started when disabled people wanted to have a say in what was being done 'to' them or 'for' them, preferring that it should be done 'with' them or, preferably, 'by' them. Their slogan, 'Nothing about us without us', summed up not only their intentions as a protest group but also their frustration at being repeatedly overlooked. Over time a different emphasis evolved, which has come to be called the social model.

But isn't it true that the medical model, despite its drawbacks, has provided the foundations on which the disability movement has built the social model? It would be an irony if that were so, as the social model is often seen to be a preferable alternative to the medical model. The development of new drugs, equipment, treatments and investigative procedures demonstrates for many the extent to which our society is willing to invest time and resources in people who previously were completely excluded from that society. Disabled people were second-class citizens for countless previous generations, and in many places they still are. But now many have a voice and take their place in society alongside others. It could be said that this is due to the way in which medicine and modern technology, far from disempowering disabled people, have given them enough stability and power to voice their own concerns and become self-advocates. Medical intervention is often essential, when looking at countries in which disabled people are the poorest of the poor.

Another important issue is that the medical model is said to be inadequate because it focuses attention only on the body. However, the fact that I have good medical care enables me to forget my body to some extent. The drugs I take mean that I can focus on the world and on my relationships with other people rather than being totally taken up with what is happening inside my head. Wheelchair users talk of their wheelchairs as being a means of liberation, not constraint.

However, if the medical profession, with its focus on the impairment of the body, were to believe that a medical response is both necessary and sufficient to explain disability, then that is a seriously inadequate view that needs challenging. Unsurprisingly, the presence of this kind of thinking in the medical profession has been the object of trenchant criticism. A radically different model of disability has been developed.

The social model

The social model arose out of the thinking and campaigning of disabled people themselves. Some of those with long-term conditions felt disempowered and alienated by the medical establishment. Acute hospital care is designed to diagnose and treat people, discharging them after they have been cured. However, many disabled people are not going to be 'cured', and the way the system worked meant that they were given the impression they were a low priority. They came into hospital a disabled person. They left a disabled person. All else was benevolent maintenance.

They also felt that they lacked control over the support networks that were set up for them; they wanted to take control of the available resources to manage their own lives. Disability was more about the problems they were confronted with in society than those they faced as a result of their impairment. In particular, these problems related to:

- environmental barriers
- social attitudes
- organizational behaviour.

Disabled people are therefore more likely to be unemployed, less likely to have physical access to infrastructure and more likely to be portrayed using negative images. Yes, someone lives with an impairment, but it is also what is done to a person that limits the way in which she can express her humanity. Within the medical model an individual is physically disadvantaged, but here she is socially disadvantaged. What is necessary is that social barriers are removed so that people can participate fully in society.

The idea that disability is generated by society meant that the disability rights movement was enabled to be much more positive. Instead of regarding themselves as deficient or tragic, disabled people could harness their anger at what has been done to them in sweeping away the barriers erected against them in society. They no longer needed charity since the denial of their human rights had become the focus of their campaign.

This perspective on disability became very powerful in society and has been instrumental in bringing about changes in legislation. The Disability Discrimination Act came onto the statute books in 1995, and this has now been superseded by the Equalities Act (2010). In the USA the Americans with Disabilities Act (1990) was heavily influenced by the ideas and lobbying of the disability rights movement.

The social model makes a clear distinction between personal and social aspects of disability: the impairment belongs to the body, while the alienation experienced is an expression of society's prejudices. From this perspective, combating disability is a political act which focuses on rights and the fight to liberate disabled people from such oppression. From seeing disability as entirely a result of problems to do with the body, it was now entirely due to society. However, this tended to lead to a view of disability where the body was ignored and with it the pain, inconvenience and struggle that can go with having an impairment.

If we are to understand disability, some of the insights in the social model are absolutely essential to take on board. This is particularly true when we come to the issues of invisibility, which we looked at earlier. While the medical perspective can sometimes reinforce stereotypes of disabled people, seeing them as having deficient bodies, distancing them from the rest of the population by categorizing them and perpetuating stereotypes, the social model has the merit of shining a spotlight on areas where disabled people are being unfairly treated. For an abled person a pavement kerb is invisible, but it becomes an obstacle for a disabled person with mobility impairments. Such hazards face disabled people all the time, as they navigate transport systems and, more generally, the built environment. In employment, despite new legislation it is much easier, and probably cheaper, for an employer to hire an abled person than to make the legally required 'reasonable adjustments' to allow an equally qualified disabled person to be appointed. The disability rights movement, using the social model, has campaigned for a recognition of the rights of disabled people, and this has resulted in significant changes in our society.

However, in the view of professor of ethics Hans Reinders, the disability rights approach to inclusion has turned it into an 'uphill battle'.

> More than anything else the disability rights movement has hammered home the claim that the notion of 'disability' is a disabling notion per se; by implication, the proper way to think about disabled people is to focus on what they can do rather than what they can't do. However, in pushing action as the rationale for its claims to equal rights and social justice, the disability rights movement has made life for the 'temporarily able-bodied' much easier than it should have been; for it has left intact their most cherished treasure, namely their self-image as 'doers' and 'achievers'. In fact, it has done nothing but reinforce that self-image.[1]

For Reinders this is convenient because abled (or in his terminology 'able-bodied') people are not being asked to change in any way. The idea that people are motivated by self-interest goes unchallenged. All we are asked to do is imagine what life would be like if we were to acquire an impairment, and then treat others as we would like to be treated. I give others their rights because one day I may need them myself. My action to obtain rights for others is still motivated by self-interest. As Reinders points out, this is not a moral obligation, unless of course someone who was motivated by moral concerns from the outset conducts the exercise. The idea that who we are is bound up with what we accomplish is left unchallenged. Disabled people may be 'included' but they are being included into a self-interested society that is already alienating its members by emphasizing autonomy and individualism. The thing that needs to be challenged is society's fixation with ambition, achievement and competition.

Reinders applies his objections to friends with intellectual disabilities.

> In endorsing the language of enlightened self-interest the disability rights movement has let me off the hook with regard to the most critical issue. In my listening to persons with intellectual disabilities, it has struck me that they long to share their lives with others, but not necessarily in the sense of being admitted, or allowed to be present as a matter of their right. They do not seek to be tolerated because of claims to equality and justice; they long to share the lives of people like me because they want to be chosen by people like me. In other words they want to belong, not on grounds of moral equality, but on the grounds of my predilection. This longing confronts us with a question that rights and justice cannot possibly address. If I am to choose a disabled person, there must be a desire on my part, a predilection on the grounds of which her presence is desirable.[2]

So the absence of friendship is key to understanding the place of disabled people in the community; however, 'it should not be surprising that the importance of friendship is rarely taken into account. Rights and justice claims have the capacity to open up public spaces, but they do not suggest what to do with them.'[3]

In common with millions of others, people with epilepsy share their hopes and dreams on internet sites and through social media. One recurrent theme is the need for friendship. Some people with epilepsy are lonely. They want friends but often lack the confidence to take the initiative to form close bonds. Yet we are no different from the rest of the population in our capacity for friendship and love. What we all know is that without love we diminish.

We are 'persons in relationship'; as we shall see in the next chapter, that statement of our human identity as 'social people' is an essential insight based on Christian doctrine. The fundamental flaw in both models – medical and social – is that they seek to separate the personal from the social. The one focuses on the body and the other on society. It is true that a new protest movement will often want to distance itself from the 'old guard' in order to make its mark, but after a while those involved may have to accept that it has claimed too much for itself.

What is necessary is for the best of both models to be integrated: the reason for this being that this is how disabled people actually see the way they live in the world. I do not distinguish between aspects of my life such as the drugs I take, my EEG tests and the social attitudes towards people with epilepsy that I come across. This is my life. It is one life, and to split it up is to detract from the way I experience it. I am disabled *both* by my impairment *and* by society.

Of course, activism is vital and society will never change if people do not stand up for their rights; but disabled people are often only able to find their voice because medicine and its associated technologies have made it possible for them to make themselves heard. Both models, when they claim independence from one another, are guilty of dualism, splitting up the world when it should be integrated. They are interdependent because we are social people. It is that interdependence that is the building block of the community.

It is also important to recognize that living in community means that we live alongside friends and family – people we love and from whom we derive energy and power. To limit the disability community to those who live with an impairment is to shut out fellow travellers who are abled but are living alongside us. It also excludes the people in the medical and other caring professions who recognize the wider needs and social barriers faced by disabled people. We cannot deny, as people living with an impairment, that we have additional or specific needs, even if they are relatively straightforward, such as a student needing handouts in a large font size because of poor vision.

One of the issues with these models of disability is that not only do they have different priorities, but they employ different tools that are essential if they are to retain their coherence as explanatory models. Medicine uses the language of science to test, diagnose and treat. The social model uses the language of politics, human rights and personal story to transform society. The question is whether these disciplines will ever come to complement or even respect each other enough to be able to work together in partnership.

What of theology? What relevance does it have to these issues? Does the Christian faith have anything distinctive to say about what it means to be a disabled person or about disability? Certainly, the Church has been the source of many effective and even radical initiatives in caring for disabled people and has campaigned for their rights as well. But it has also been the source of great misery for disabled people, providing theological justification for ill treatment and abuse, and has much to answer for. Hopefully, the current Christian perspective on disability is liberating and affirming. It is to the major themes of the Christian faith that we now turn, asking how they illumine the key questions with which we are faced.

In the following chapters we will be looking at four great building blocks of the Christian faith, which I call creation, compromise, covenant and completion. Think of these four themes as lenses through which we look on the world. We need all four to be able to see the world clearly. Christianity claims that it represents truth; if so, we will be able, using these four themes, to expose the false assumptions that oppress disabled people, as well as provide the basis for a completely different way of understanding what it means to be a person.

We start where it all began, with creation. If we do not know what God's original intentions were then we have nothing against which to measure our lives now.

4

Creation

The Bible throws down the gauntlet with its first four words: 'In the beginning God'. Arguments about how the universe was made will never end, it seems, but this statement lies outside the evolution debate. Whatever the means God used to make the universe, this statement is categorical in claiming that it is God who is the source of creation, and that everything that exists comes from God's imagination. We are those who are the created, so it matters who God is because that is the biggest clue as to who we are and how we can understand each other.

Perhaps the greatest hint as to who we are is given when Genesis talks of our being made 'in the image of God'. When Christians speak of 'the image of God' in the context of disability, they are often discussing the nature of personhood – what it means to be a person. God's statement, 'Let us make human beings in our image' (Gen. 1.26) is fundamental to a Christian perspective of who we are as a human race. All things were brought into being through God's intention and crafted according to God's imagination. So there is divine purpose at the heart of the universe.

Science, in seeking to answer the question 'How?', currently traces our origins to the 'big bang'. Theology, looking for an answer to the question 'Why?', places us in the hands of an imaginative creator. Whatever the scientific story of beginnings turns out to be, it does not interfere with the theological story, apart from the fact that theology insists that those beginnings were not the impersonal, random product of chance but a personal, purposeful act of the imagination.

Science looks to human reason to explain not only how the universe functions, but also our own identity, since we are indistinguishable from the universe. Reason is a powerful tool when used appropriately, but in the same way that science and faith ask different questions about our origins, so from a theological perspective reason cannot form the essential foundation of human identity. It must always be combined with faith.

In Genesis 1.26 it is God the Trinity (Father, Son and Holy Spirit) who is speaking: 'Let *us* make human beings in *our* image.' The concept of the image of God is notoriously difficult to pin down, but it seems reasonable to suggest that it has a Trinitarian foundation. Elements of the creation narrative support this. Events in the Garden of Eden, which is not only a paradise teeming with life but a story replete with meaning, provide the context for this. God has pronounced the creation 'good' and the world is full of life of every kind. A human body is made of dust, but even before things go disastrously wrong in Genesis 3 this 'dust body' is pronounced 'not good'.

This seemingly damning indictment in the midst of all that is otherwise good results from the absence of human relationships. God clarifies this by adding, 'It is not good for the man *to be alone.*' In the story the animals are brought before Adam but none is found to be adequate as a companion. This inadequacy shows that Adam has a need for someone who shares his perspective on life, and is capable of conversation, mutuality and love. He has been made for relationship and it is not present. The world is waiting with anticipation for a further act of creation. The world is good but it is not *complete*.

However, there is a deeper reason than loneliness for this inadequacy. Humanity was brought into being by a God who is three persons in relationship. God is love (1 John 4.7–21), and that love flows between the three persons of the Trinity. In that love we find the true picture of what it means to be in relationship. We exist because the inner love of God overflows in the act of our creation. Adam, the person of dust, was inadequate; he could not represent the image of God because he was not a 'person in relationship', as is the Trinity. This insight provides us with the idea that it is the *relational*, not the *rational*, that provides the foundation for human identity.

It is relationship with God that Christianity sees as foundational to human identity, not only because it is God who creates the universe and pronounces it 'good', but because in declaring Adam's loneliness as 'not good' God relates to humanity and understands our needs in a fundamental way. God sees us. In providing friendship and love for us, God shows that our relationship is about everything that is needed for human flourishing. We can go further than that and say that God's original intention was that we should experience joy in creation, but experience it *together*.

When it comes to our relationship with other people, we find that the creation narrative is a good guide to understanding ourselves. The solution to Adam's loneliness is the creation of the woman, Eve. When Adam sees Eve for the first time he says, 'This is now bone of my bones and flesh of my flesh; she shall be called "woman", for she was taken out of man' (Gen. 2.23).

Two elements here are fundamental to what it means to be in relationship together. The first is *recognition*, the second is *respect*. In Eve, Adam recognizes what he did not find in any of the animals – a common humanity. This person is human. She experiences life as a human being. She is able to complement Adam in a way that is mutual. This is the end of loneliness. Adam respects Eve. She is the same as him in her humanity but she is different from him because she is woman and he is man. They are both human, but Eve has a different experience of being human. Conversation and creativity are possible because she does not replicate the man but is differentiated from him. He is called to respect her difference and treat her life as equal with his own. In fact, this need for both recognition and respect runs through every human relationship, not just that initial relationship between the first man and woman. A healthy community depends on the essential balancing act of recognizing common humanity and respecting difference. When we 'put away' disabled people, or talk to their carers over their heads, we lose that balance between recognition and respect and we deny them their humanity.

Adam has found another human being and he is filled with joy. It is the creator's intention that human relationships are to be celebrated. They are at the heart of human flourishing. We acquire dignity as human beings by being made in the image of God. But the image of God is not just at the heart of creation; it is essential to our calling as a human community. That calling is to look for the image of God in others.

A society that is individualistic and 'selfist' will implode because it loses the desire to see other people as God sees us. Indeed, the response to Adam's loneliness is a judgement on individualism as the essential building block of the modern world. The idea that we are called to moderate our pace in order to take notice of others and celebrate their stories is lost in a fast-changing world; our interest in others is focused on the degree to which they have power, affluence or celebrity. As the prodigal son found, for example, nobody wanted to know him after his wealth had gone. There was little left of him when his relationships atrophied and he ended up in a pigsty eating with the pigs. When we have more than enough, we can become blind to the possibility that we are making do with a distorted and dysfunctional view of the world. If that world were to collapse around our ears and we became impoverished, we would have little to live with but the regret that we were never attentive to others, and the fear that we may lose everything we are. In short, our sense of our own value disappears as power declines. Instead we are to slow down to the extent that we notice others and can explore what it means for them to be made in the image of God. In some cases, where they are very different from us, that may take time. Time focused on others is time well spent.

A duty to deny life?

If reason is at the heart of human identity, what of those who are completely unable to exercise reason, or can do so only to a limited extent or intermittently? A person with severe learning difficulties or dementia could be said not to exercise reason, or not to the satisfaction of a fast-moving competitive society. Unborn children are also incapable of exercising reason. There have certainly been periods in history where 'absence of reason' has been cited to legitimize acts of slavery, enforced incarceration or infanticide. Indeed, how are we to understand personhood when it is applied to people with profound intellectual disabilities? They are human because they are of human origins, but how can we describe their potential when the goal of human existence is understood as reaching one's full potential through the application of reason?[1]

The German theologian Dietrich Bonhoeffer captured the essence of a Christian view of creatureliness:

> Life created and preserved by God possesses an inherent right; completely independent of its social utility . . . There is no worthless life before God, because God holds life itself to be valuable. Because God is the Creator, Preserver and Redeemer of life, even the poorest life before God becomes a valuable life.[2]

In the view of some commentators, our consumer society is turning people themselves into objects of consumption. They see us entering a new phase, with eugenics waiting in the wings while it is debated whether or not the lives of some people are worth preserving, given the limited resources we have at our disposal. Our liberal society values freedom of choice above almost anything else; when genetic testing offers prospective parents an array of options based on information about the foetus, we regard that choice as a good thing. The problem is that a liberal society, which elevates freedom of choice to one of its primary values, does not necessarily indicate which choices are good ones. So the use of such information will depend on the moral vision of the society in which it is received or the personal moral convictions of those involved.

In a society where this information is available, and where people with profound intellectual impairments are viewed negatively, the willingness to choose to have a child with such impairments will depend increasingly on the moral convictions of parents. A liberal society that only goes as far as to say that choice is good fails its people when it cannot indicate which choices are good ones. It may have no way of protecting its weakest members, as the choice to abort is seen as entirely reasonable and even encouraged in a world of scarce resources.

Parents of disabled children sometimes tell of the pressure that was exerted on them by doctors to end the pregnancy, when it was discovered that the foetus had an impairment. We seem to have moved a long way – from access to abortion (following the legislation of 1967), through the right to have an abortion (as a result of the campaigning of the women's movement in the late twentieth century), to a situation where there sometimes appears to be a duty to abort. If so, this is a chilling development and one that I discuss with Jean Vanier later in this book.

In his book *The Future of the Disabled in Liberal Society*,[3] Hans Reinders talks of exactly this. He foresees a day when prospective parents who knowingly continue with the pregnancy and birth of a disabled child will be informed that they are entitled to no benefits from the state as they have ignored advice to abort the foetus. At the end of the day, a materialistic society whose moral vision has atrophied finds that it is dehumanized by denying life to those individuals it regards as taking up too many resources or causing too much inconvenience. We are left with a society of extreme self-centredness that gradually loses sight of what it means to be human. This is what is meant by the tyranny of normality. In this case it has become extreme.

We need to remember in all this that we are *persons* in *relationship*. These two elements, when kept in tension with one another, are the irreducible minimum of human identity. We cannot label ourselves as autonomous individuals; indeed, there is no such concept in the Christian tradition because the personal is founded on the Trinitarian. We are persons but live in relationship. We cannot be defined by either the one or the other. The application of reason suggests that we must choose, but at the heart of this tension is a mystery. It is the mystery of the Trinity. There is only one God, but this one God is three persons in one.

What social expectations derive from this insight? Far from the supposed norm of autonomy, by which human behaviour is judged in contemporary society, this leads us towards interdependence, built on the foundations of recognition and respect. The glue that holds this together is trust. Trust in God and trust in others.

We trust most of all that God is 'for us'. John Swinton eloquently expresses what this means for the person with dementia.

> If, in Christ, God has opened up his very being in relationship to human beings, there is nothing that can change this transformative fact; not neurological deterioration, not forgetting who and whose we are, nothing. God remains with and for the person with dementia even when the person can no longer be with and for God, at least in a cognitive sense. The significance and personhood of the person with dementia is safeguarded and sustained within the very being of God quite apart from the relationships a person may or may encounter at a temporal level. We might forget God, but God will not and, indeed, cannot forget us. When we can no longer minister to God and to others, the God who is with us and for us will minister to us in our hour of need.[4]

So what makes us human? God *created* us, God *sees* us. God is *for* us. It is this that we recognize in others, and this that we are called to celebrate in our relationships. To say that we are made 'in the image of God' is not just a statement about the status and nature of humanity. It is an invitation to explore that 'image' in other people, and for that to happen we must first be interested in one another and earn the right to listen to the stories of other people.

If we are 'social persons' because God is a social person, then others hold part of our identity. We do not possess the only key to who we are, because we are known by other people. Consider what happens when we go on a holiday. We come back with stories about what we have done, and also about others who were there. Over time we may relate the same events, but miss out an enormous amount of detail, so we never tell the entire story. Those who were with us have their own story to tell. But they also have some of ours. They can provide coinciding memories and correct our versions of others. Like finding old photos in a scrapbook, we are reminded of who we once were, rediscovering a part of our identity that we had forgotten.

Because we respect each other's stories, we have an obligation to one another to use those stories to remind each other of our common humanity. We *see* each other, we *hold* each other. When a person has dementia, for instance, her memories of the past may fade. But we who know her story have an obligation to help her to remember who she is. Our respect for her is based on the fact that we are 'persons in relationship'. Even when she does not respond to us, it is an act of faith that she is still present; we should continue to talk, sing and walk with her until her story is complete.

The disappearing body

One reason why relationship alone cannot be the source of the whole story regarding identity is our need for a theology of the body. In talking about disability it is essential to take the body seriously. All too often in theology the body has been ignored, the focus being on the 'soul' or the 'spirit'. The body is relegated, regarded as an obstacle that gets in way of what God is doing in the world, or even as the source of those temptations and evils to which humanity is prey. But if we are to have a complete view of what it means to be embodied we must start with creation. Our perceptions of each other's bodies affect our human relationships, just as the nature of our human relationships affect our perceptions of each other's bodies.

The severity of our impairments will have an impact on those perceptions. This may lead to a reduction in self-esteem; a person with an impairment may well be aware that he is perceived differently, and feel that he has a reduced opportunity for fulfilling human relationships just because of how others perceive him. But one of the extraordinary things about friendship is that how we look begins to have much less of an impact on how we perceive one another. The body is important. As we shall see, the incarnation of Jesus shows us just how important the body is.

Perhaps the first thing to note about the creation narrative and its attitude to the body is its emphasis on our 'creatureliness'. God breathes into Adam and he becomes a 'living soul', but he is also a creature. There is a connection with the earth, an 'earthiness' that goes with being a person. When Adam names all the animals but finds no companion, he discovers that he is fundamentally different. The other animals have companions of their own species in order to procreate. Adam is embodied but unique.

It is important to recognize two other things before we continue. Adam is both *vulnerable* and *susceptible*. He is vulnerable in that he is the only one without a suitable companion and since he was made for such companionship he is *unfinished*. This points to Eden being a fragile place. It was placed on the earth by God for a specific purpose – as a setting for the great drama to unfold. The rest of the earth needed managing even though it was a fruitful environment. True, the creation is pro-nounced 'good'. But it is also a place where Adam is alone, where the animals are inadequate helpers, where the tempter is present and where both Adam and Eve are susceptible to mistrust without any foundation. There is only one portrayal of the perfect society in the Scriptures, and it is not Eden the garden – it is the New World, as we shall see later on in this book.

Theologian Tom Reynolds outlines another reason why human beings are vulnerable, and that is because we are embodied. To be embodied is to be finite, to be open to disease, trauma and disability. This vulnerability is part of what it means to be human. No one can escape it. We cannot characterize disabled people as being vulnerable and the rest of the population as invulnerable. Vulnerability is a characteristic of the whole of humanity. That is why, as Reynolds points out, interdependence, and not independence and autonomy, is the more accurate description of what it means to be human.[5]

As we will see in the next chapter, this vulnerable body and these vital relationships have been compromised, and God grapples with humanity to bring about his purposes. The angels posted at the gates of Eden with flaming swords mean that history will go in only one direction. There is no going back to Eden. If humanity is to rediscover what it means to be made in the image of God, the answer must lie in the future.

5

Compromise

———◆———

An elderly lady in a wheelchair is sunning herself in the park while her friend goes into the nearby shops. She is living with multiple sclerosis, which is in its advanced stages. Her reverie is disturbed when a young man she has never met comes up to her and says, 'You must have done something very wrong to be in this state.' Her friend returns to find her weeping.

This story illustrates not only ignorance, awe-inspiring rudeness and callous behaviour, but an attitude that lurks just beneath the surface of even the most civilized society – that there is some kind of link between 'sin' and disability. That young man obviously believed that people are impaired because they have done something wrong.

It could, of course, be true in some cases. A person could drink and drive, have an accident and as a result live with a permanent impairment. There is then a direct link between wrongdoing and impairment. In some kinds of chaotic lifestyles we may see a direct relationship between wrongdoing and disability. Dependency on alcohol or drugs, or some sexual addictions, can lead to acquiring an impairment. The appropriate response is not to declare judgement, however, but to offer help.

But that is not what is meant here. The idea is that a scientific or medical explanation is not enough. What is needed is an explanation rooted in spirituality. The irony is that such a callous approach is used by people who often have no interest in spiritual things themselves. It could be described as the ultimate put-down. It consists of two parts: what had happened to her was bad, not only physically but morally, and the reason for it happening was that she was being judged.

It's often not easy to shake off this kind of approach. I find it hard when people suggest that my epilepsy is demon-possession. There are three elements at play here that make dealing with such accusations difficult.

First, it is the outcome of fractured relationships. Friendship is about knowing and being known. Relationships of recognition and respect go beyond stereotyping and accusation and seek to affirm and build up. Making an accusation like this is not the act of a friend. The person who can wound and then walk on in such a way is the opposite of the friend, 'who sticks closer than a brother' (Prov. 18.24). The book of Proverbs can even envisage a situation where a friend may have something to tell us that we will not like, but says that 'Wounds from a friend can be trusted' (Prov. 27.6). Even when we have to say difficult things to one another, we are more able to do this when we are faithful friends who desire the best for one another and who trust one another. This jarring episode in the life of a gracious elderly lady is the very opposite of that. It is an illustration of the young man's perception of the difference between 'us' and 'them'.

Second, she is not told what she has done wrong. The situation is bad enough, but perhaps she could have got to grips with it if her supposed 'sin' had been specified. But the accusation, despite being aggressive, is ephemeral. Presumably the young man believes this about everybody with an impairment, at least one that is overt. One wonders whether it would ever occur to him that his own wrongdoing could be said to be leading to his having an impairment. If it did, he would not be so casual in wounding others. As will be seen later, the Church itself sometimes wounds people in this way. After 'healing prayer' yields no results people may be asked whether there is sin in their life that is blocking their healing.[1] One wonders which context is the more damning, the park or the chancel.

Third, his remark appeals to her own fear. There is a fear in every human being that needs to be dealt with if it is not to become a burden to us. Buried deep within us is the idea that when we are going through difficult times we have in fact displeased God (or in some cultures 'the gods') in some way; what we are experiencing is a sign that we are to blame for something, although we cannot put our finger on what it may be. It is the existence of this voice in our heads, however intermittent and softly spoken, that makes such an accusation so unfair. How many millions of people have asked, 'Why am I going through this? I live a decent life. I don't deserve this.' We are fragile people and the idea that we are impaired because of sin, especially sin for which we are said to be responsible, prevents us from experiencing that joy in our creation that was the intention of the Creator.

A problem with Scripture?

When people want to draw attention to the way in which Christianity has harmed the reputation of disabled people they often cite the pervasive idea of perfection in Scripture. God is perfect and seems to require perfection of us. Surely, then, God is prejudiced against impairment? But none of us can measure up to perfection. If we restrict this shortcoming as predominantly applicable to disabled people, all we have done is assert our idea of normality once more. Instead of counting everybody as falling short of God's standards, we have yet again applied it to disabled people in particular. None of us knows what it means to be perfect, but we tend to stick to the standard that reflects best on us, which is that God accepts those who are 'normal', and has a problem with those with an impairment.

It is true that there are some scriptural contexts in which God requires ritual perfection. In a sacrifice, the offering of the lamb or goat must be 'unblemished'. An impaired priest cannot officiate in the Holy Place (although he can eat the holy bread). Yet there are many other restrictions on who is admitted or denied access to these particular rituals and situations. There is no suggestion that either disability or poverty is necessarily a falling short of perfection. Indeed God calls on Israel to take care of those who are in need.

So in what is God perfect? God is transcendent above all things and certainly beyond comparisons. God is utterly holy. God is absolutely faithful and trustworthy. God is committed to truth and love. That love is seen in the beauty of creation. God is perfect in justice and in compassion for the poor. That is what we mean when we say God is perfect. Because of this God is dependable. Over thousands of years people have prayed expectantly, believing in God's 'holy character'. God cannot contradict himself. Last, we know that this Old Testament God comes in the person of Jesus to show us what God is like in human form. As we will see, both Old and New Testaments see God as the champion of the poor and oppressed.

While the language of perfection may be the first problem people have with Scripture, the second is the language of judgement. On occasion the Bible uses disability as the consequence of judgement. For instance, Zechariah, the husband of Elizabeth and prospective father of John the Baptist, does not believe the message of the angel Gabriel when told that his elderly wife will become pregnant (Luke 1.20). As a result he is rendered mute until the baby is born. Such actions are found at several points throughout Scripture.

Disabling language is not the only form of judgement, however. Death, poverty, famine and military defeat are all used in similar ways. Israel was comprehensively defeated because it disobeyed God, as in 1 Samuel 4. God then revealed what had happened, so they were able to right the wrong. In 1 Kings 8 the Ark of the Covenant is brought into the temple, and King Solomon prays, dedicating the temple. In his prayer he lists the things that could go wrong because the people are disobedient to God and asks that God will have mercy and restore them, if the people repent.

So what is it about the link between sin and disability? In a world where 100 per cent of people die, you would have thought that death would be the main focus. But death is viewed as a natural phenomenon, whereas in many cultures disability apparently has a link with sin or evil. Perhaps that is it. The fact that all of us die is seen as belonging to the world of the normal. We say 'death is a part of life'. Death is regrettable but has become invisible. We prefer not to talk about it. We fear it, we are anxious about it, but can do nothing about it. We may see disability as the next rung on the same ladder. It is visible but fewer people experience it. Yet we still fear disability as a possible future for ourselves. In a world where we seek to control our prospects and our identity, we don't want to be reminded of our vulnerability, however powerful we are.

A false sense of security

We exist in this compromised world by clutching on to a false sense of security. Genesis 3 presents a vivid story of a betrayal of trust. The Garden of Eden was a place created to be a backdrop for a great drama, one that revolved around trust in God. Everything was permitted except eating from one tree. The existence of that one constraint defined what it meant to trust God. Eat from it and the trust was broken. Accept what God said and the trust remained. We all know how the tragedy unfolded. Eating from the tree meant that Adam and Eve 'had their eyes opened'. Instead of living in God's way they now had to decide how to live for themselves. The problem was that their perception of themselves and of the world was now distorted.

They realized that they were naked. Before they had gloried in their bodies; now they tried to cover them up. They hid from the presence of God. They blamed each other for what had happened. Shame, guilt and anxiety accompanied the event, all flowing from the basic mistrust in what God had said.

The problem then was how to live in the light of this. The security of trust in God had gone. What other security was there in the world? Realizing they were naked, they made clothes. They began to control their environment. As time went on, relationships between them changed. An egalitarian partnership between the man and the woman became suffused with power (Gen. 3.16). Things sank to a new low when their sons Cain and Abel competed for God's approval and Abel was killed as a result.

The quest for new forms of security and control was not restricted to the personal and relational. Genesis 11 tells the story of the tower of Babel. A group of people conspired to defeat the purposes of God by using new technology to build a tower. They wanted to make a name for themselves. Yet, again, they were not prepared to believe that God's way was the best way. As a result they were scattered by God and their lust for power was dissipated.

This is a tragic story of fractured relationships and a lust for power born out of anxiety. Even the land itself plays a part in the growth of this anxiety. Before this, although it needed management the world was fruitful. But afterwards resources became scarce and competition for those resources escalated.

All this started because humanity couldn't accept that there were limits to what it meant to be human. It was not understood that humanity is necessarily vulnerable and that people need one another. So many of the issues we struggle with have been born from that ferment.

The concept of Eden is largely about hospitality. It is a place of welcome – but we have rejected that welcome. We have turned away, and we have created a world where competitiveness, ambition and the desire to accumulate wealth have meant that some people are marginalized, and their welcome is damaged or destroyed. We have created not only a 'normal body' but a 'normal world'. But those who can most accurately see its dysfunction and delusion are those who have been pushed to the margins. Is the best that we can offer disabled people that they should be integrated into such a world and conform to its values and behaviour in the name of accessing power? To do so is to give up the possibility of becoming prophets to it, or, more cunningly, those who subvert it – showing, as St Paul said, a better way (1 Cor. 12.31).

Living with sadness

In a compromised world we also live with sadness. But because of our frenzied quest for security and control we treat sadness as a foreign body that needs to be repelled. Yet we cannot live without it as it is a vital part of living in a compromised world. We need to relearn sadness. Billions are invested in the pharmaceutical industry to keep sadness at bay, and therapies of numerous kinds prosper from our anxiety to rid ourselves of it. For some, such therapies provide welcome relief, while others suffer in silence.

Sadness in the form of depression has dark corners and depths where we can become entrapped. Those of us who have found ourselves in the dark with no means of escape need help to rediscover even the smallest glimmer of light. People who live through periods of depression find that the condition is still stigmatized in our society. It is a matter for conjecture whether the Church is at all successful in helping those in such darkness. The disabling society puts pressure on those with mental health problems to feel that they are not 'normal', in much the same way as those with physical impairments, if not more so. Yet one in four adults in the UK will experience a mental health problem in any given year, with nine out of ten of them saying that they have experienced discrimination because of it.[2] Mental health issues go to the core of our identity and self-esteem, and undermine our view of ourselves as socially acceptable people.

It may seem churlish to turn to theology in the face of such human agony, but there is real help here. Ironically, this is often ignored by the Church itself. One reason for this is that in emphasizing the living of a happy life as the normal expression of the Christian existence, the Church has made itself less relevant to those who are not enjoying life to the requisite extent. A Church that regards happiness as the norm has little if anything to say to those who are engulfed by darkness. Yet many of us will experience such darkness at some point in our lives.

The wasted area is that of 'lament' – to be found in the Psalms in particular. The psalmist grapples with sadness, rage and disappointment, emotions that seem to be unacceptable to some Christians, although they would perhaps be allowed if everything comes right in the last verse. But all too often we are left with pain and questioning as to where God is, and this too is a part of what it means to be human. The Psalms of Lament give us permission to be angry, and to question God without fear of retribution. Even Jesus cried out in his despair on the cross: 'Father, why have you deserted me?' There was no answer. It should be comforting to know that we can rage at God and be honest about the pain of the world. We know that the cavalry does not necessarily come over the hill to rescue the troops in the last verse. Yet we do rage 'in hope', and the reason why we can do this is the subject of the next chapter.

6

Covenant

Humanity has been expelled from the garden and faces a new, unknown world, in which choices have to be made and trust is at a premium. Good and bad, right and wrong are intertwined, and it seems that no guidance has been given as to how to choose well. Humanity is totally unprepared. This is a world where there is abuse of power and in which exclusion and discrimination are ever-present, but also where celebration, blessing and choosing the good are still possible. Fundamentally, humanity has chosen to make its own way in the world, and bears the burden of distrusting God in the name of freedom.

Yet this world is not devoid of the presence of God. From the moment the man and woman choose to go their own way, God begins to grapple with the human story to bring about his purposes. Throughout history God shows people how they can live in a way that both pleases him and sustains the well-being of the community.

God's love is seen in the way he unconditionally takes the initiative to enter into covenant agreements with individuals, families, nations and with humanity itself. God regards these as binding promises on his part to which humanity must respond. As in the garden, we are free to obey and find blessing, or go our own way and suffer the consequences. But we are created to cooperate with God, not compete with him. At the heart of these covenants God reveals something of his own holy character and states what he requires of others in return. This exchange of *revelation* and *requirement* becomes a key factor in the rhythm of the biblical narrative as it unfolds. The idea that 'you become what you worship' is illustrated in the way that idolatry brings cruelty and has to be expunged. Conversely, to worship the true God is to become a holy people who love to do what is right.

As the theologian Christopher Wright has pointed out, God sets out the norms by which people should live if they are to experience *shalom*. Personal and social well-being can be found in a world that threatens to overturn relationships and undermine communities. Usually translated 'peace', *shalom* goes far beyond the absence of violence or war, or even the presence of rest and safety. It describes the restoration of right relationships in which the people, the land and God are in harmony. Israel, called into existence by God's covenant with Abraham, will be able to achieve this by following 'the way of the Lord'. In other words, Israel is to imitate God's ways. These values are completely different from those of the surrounding nations and reflect God's passion for justice. Israel is called to ethical behaviour that is not based on rules and regulations but on emulating the character of God.

Poverty and oppression

Before turning specifically to disability, it is important to look briefly at the Old Testament perspective on poverty. It is in this context and on this foundation that attitudes to disability can be understood.

Throughout Scripture God is revealed as having a passionate concern for the poor and oppressed. There is an obligation to respond to the presence of poverty, and, in a community where right relationships are paramount, to respond ethically. How a person has come to be in poverty is for another day, although the Bible has some sharp words about people who are poor because they are lazy or dishonest. But people cannot be persistently poor if God's portrayal of Israel as a flourishing community, living in *shalom*, is to be a reality. This could be achieved through the way resources, such as land, were attached to the family, interest on loans was banned and land that had been lost was returned in the year of jubilee.

Yet a welfare programme is also described that meant that those who had no land or family were provided for. Christopher Wright outlines these as follows:[1]

- The right of gleaning at harvest time (Exod. 23.10–11; Deut. 24.18–22).
- The triennial tithe, out of which 10 per cent went to provide a social fund for the needy (Deut. 14.28–29).
- The sabbatical year, in which crops from fallow land became available (Exod. 23.10–11).
- The cancellation (or suspension) of debts (Deut. 15.1–11).
- The freeing of Hebrew slaves (Deut. 15.12–18).

In addition, the poor were to be treated as equals before the law, and crucially, it is those possessing power and wealth who are addressed when issues relating to poverty are discussed. Far from poor people being told to sort themselves out, it is those with the wherewithal to do something about the situation who are told to act. Finally, as Wright points out, referring to the book of Deuteronomy, caring for the poor should be the litmus test of obedience to the whole of the rest of the law.

> Thus giving to the needy is not only a sacred duty to God but it also is the defining point for any claim to have kept the law. *The law is kept only if the poor are cared for.* Only when Israel responds to the needy by enabling everyone in the community to eat and be satisfied can they affirm 'I have done everything that you commanded me.' This shows . . . how the enacted love for the poor and needy is the practical proof of genuine God-honouring love for the neighbour. The Torah itself thus agrees with the way the prophets later pinpoint and prioritize care for the poor as somehow definitive or paradigmatic of Israel's response to God as a whole.[2]

It was essential to this that poor people were seen and not ignored. They could not be relegated to the margins of society if responding to their needs was central to the uniqueness of Israel. To overlook the needs of poor people would be a declaration of Israel's spiritual poverty.

Disability must be read in this context. It is true that attitudes to disability change as the biblical narrative progresses, in the same way as those towards women or slaves changed over time.[3] It is also true that some attitudes in the Bible are difficult to interpret. The way in which the Bible uses words associated with impairment in connection with God's judgement could be seen as an illustration of the Old Testament's negative attitude to disability. But these metaphorical allusions, or real actions, do not sum up the Bible's central theme on these issues. Attitudes towards disabled people should imitate those of the God of justice. God identifies with them in a fundamental way: 'Do not curse the deaf or put a stumbling block in front of the blind, but fear your God. I am the Lord' (Lev. 19.14).

The way in which attitudes to the poor and needy are used as criteria for judgement is most powerfully expressed by Jesus, when he speaks of people ignoring the needs of others: the hungry, the thirsty, the stranger, needing clothes, being sick or in prison.

> For I was hungry and you gave me nothing to eat, I was thirsty and you gave me nothing to drink, I was a stranger and you did not invite me in, I needed clothes and you did not clothe me, I was sick and in prison and you did not look after me. They also will answer, 'Lord, when did we see you hungry or thirsty or a stranger or needing clothes or sick or in prison, and did not help you?' He will reply, 'Truly I tell you, whatever you did not do for one of the least of these, you did not do for me.'
>
> (Matt. 25.40–45)

Indeed, we are to be advocates for those who cannot speak for themselves: 'Speak up for those who cannot speak for themselves, for the rights of all who are destitute. Speak up and judge fairly; defend the rights of the poor and needy' (Prov. 31.8–9).

A society cannot live in *shalom* if it ignores those in need, or treats them unequally before the law. In fact, to abuse disabled people, or even to ignore them, is to have to deal with God, to risk judgement. These are not just matters of social nicety but go to the heart of what it means to be a 'good society'. We can say from this evidence that a society is judged not on how it creates opportunities for the wealthy but on how it treats those who are poor.

Yet from the beginning of this book it has been clear that disabled people are not 'seen' by those in power. They are rendered invisible, and not drawn into relationship. Of course, rights for disabled people have improved, and we can say that they have become more equal before the law. But this equality is not *personal*. It is not about *people*. The advent of disability rights has not delivered *love*. Political systems may talk the language of justice but they can never deliver love. Only people create love.

The medical model focuses on the physical body. The rights model focuses on the political body. What is needed is the missing *person*. It is this vacuum that the biblical picture seeks to fill. It is primarily concerned with covenantal relationships in which the character of the community is determined by the character of God, and which reflect the gracious offer of friendship by God.

The coming of Jesus

In the Incarnation, Jesus came to show us what God is like in human form. He came to *reveal* the character of God, and to show us how to live according to what God *requires*. In the Gospels, his public ministry opens with his declaration in his local synagogue that the prophecies concerning the coming of the Messiah in the Old Testament are fulfilled in him.

> The Spirit of the Lord is upon me, because he has anointed
> me to proclaim good news to the poor. He has sent me to pro-
> claim freedom for the prisoners and recovery of sight for
> the blind, to set the oppressed free, to proclaim the year of the
> Lord's favour. (Luke 4.18–19)

On another occasion, the disciples of John the Baptist come to ask whether he is in fact the Messiah, or whether they should continue to wait for him to come. Jesus responds: 'Go back and report to John what you hear and see: The blind receive sight, the lame walk, those who have leprosy are cleansed, the deaf hear, the dead are raised, and the good news is proclaimed to the poor' (Matt. 11.4–5).

Disabled people are at the very heart of the ministry of Jesus. Not only did he associate with them, he was willing to defy the socio-political boundaries of his day in order to be with them. Whether it was defying cultural attitudes by touching lepers, breaking religious regulations by healing on the Sabbath, or defiling himself by touching a dead body, Jesus cared more about the person than he did about the system although he frequently challenged those who used their political and religious power to oppress others. Jesus was also well aware of the contemporary view that disability was a result of sin – a view that is not far under the surface in the modern world, and still prevalent in other parts of the world.

Certainly, Job's 'comforters' in the Old Testament mistakenly saw his afflictions as stemming from something he had done that had incurred the wrath of God. It is possible to gain the impression that the Bible sees disability as a problem with the body that is part of a suffering world; the resolution to this is either continued suffering, healing, or the wait to be physically changed in the next life. The story of the man born blind in John's Gospel is something of an antidote to such a monochrome view of Scripture.

In John 9 a man who was born blind is brought before Jesus. The fact that the man did not acquire the impairment during his life prompts the disciples to ask Jesus, 'who sinned, this man or his parents?' Their assumption was that there was a direct and symbolic link between sin and impairment. Jesus states that neither the man nor his parents had sinned. His blindness was so 'that the works of God might be displayed in him' (9.3). Colleen Grant says of this, 'whereas the disciples are interested in the past cause of the man's blindness, Jesus speaks of its future purpose'.[4]

Disabled people are frequently associated with imperfection, sin and inadequacy. It entraps them in a false identity. It perpetuates the unanswerable question, 'What have I done to deserve this?' Jesus cuts across this by liberating the man to enjoy the future. In what follows, the healing itself seems to be secondary to the way in which the man who was formerly blind behaves. It is true that part of his liberation comes from his healing – a healing he did not ask for but was granted nonetheless. The rest of the passage consists of his defence of Jesus when he is confronted by neighbours and religious officials. He comes across as a strong character capable of great irony and humour. This is not a picture of some weak, passive individual who cowers away from society. Those arguing with him define him by his blindness, but this is not how he sees himself. Colleen Grant comments:

> Jesus began by stating that the man was born blind so that God's works might be revealed in him. As the story progresses we discover that this revelation goes far beyond the healing of his disability. Significantly, the work of God is even evident in the man's gradually increasing faith and conviction before the opponents of Jesus. Indeed, I would argue that even more than in Jesus' act of healing, the work of God is the man's role as witness to Jesus. In this sense it is not the man's blindness or his healing which is essential to the story.[5]

This man has been discriminated against because he has been defined by his being blind. Having been healed, he explodes on to the stage – Jesus disappears while the action is happening. In our age this man would be a cross between a barrister and a satirist.

He illustrates what it means to be discriminated against, and also how it feels to be defined by one's impairment. Both are examples of a compromised world in which people are not treated as God intended them to be. John 9 illustrates the difference between healing and cure. The man's blindness was cured, but his life was healed as well. He discovered well-being and recovered his true identity. We will return to this theme later in the book.

Yet people did not have to be cured of their impairments in order to celebrate what it means to enjoy the life of the kingdom of God. Jesus tells of a wealthy man who was throwing a party. He invites his wealthy and influential friends, only to find that they turn him down, giving various excuses as to why they cannot come. Becoming annoyed, the man tells his servant, 'Go out quickly into the streets and alleys of the town and bring in the poor, the crippled, the blind and the lame' (Luke 14.15–24).

Jesus tells this story to reinforce the point that we shouldn't do things just for people who can repay us, but also for people who cannot. The parable is told in response to somebody saying, 'Blessed are those who will eat at the feast in the kingdom of God' (Luke 14.15). It does not end with the party-giver inviting another group of his wealthy friends. Jesus lived alongside those who were viewed by society as 'unworthy'. Jesus' invitation is unconditional. You are accepted as you are. Some are even compelled to accept the invitation. The kingdom of God, unlike some areas of the Christian Church, celebrates diversity in all its exhilarating glory.

The disabled God

The Gospels tell us that people followed Jesus around in their thousands. Some came to him for what they thought Jesus could do for them. Some of them loved him. Opponents plotted to bring him down. Yet his story shows the extraordinary extent to which he experienced the alienation, discrimination and injustice felt by millions throughout human history. Isaiah's vision of the suffering servant was a portrayal of the Jesus who was to come hundreds of years later:

> He had no beauty or majesty to attract us to him, nothing in his appearance that we should desire him. He was despised and rejected by mankind, a man of suffering, and familiar with pain. Like one from whom people hide their faces he was despised, and we held him in low esteem. Surely he took up our pain and bore our suffering, yet we considered him punished by God, stricken by him, and afflicted. But he was pierced for our transgressions, he was crushed for our iniquities; the punishment that brought us peace was on him, and by his wounds we are healed. (Isa. 53.2b−5)

If this is a prophetic reference to Jesus, then the idea that the only person in the history of the world who was morally perfect would also be physically perfect seems to be a non-starter. Indeed he was despised and rejected, as 'one from whom people hide their faces'. The picture is a powerful one – of people crossing the street and with cloaks covering their faces in order to avoid him. Here is a person who understands discrimination because he has been discriminated against: a 'man of suffering, and familiar with pain'.

In this context, there are people in the world today who physically suffer more than Jesus did, perhaps living with intolerable pain every day of their lives. They may be trapped in a body that cannot communicate, with no prospect of improvement. Others may live with mental health issues that seem never-ending, stretching out before them for decades to come. What price a few hours on a cross? In modern torture there are ways that a person can be kept in agony for years before death envelops them.

Yet Jesus identifies with us in our suffering and oppression, as a victim of injustice and an outcast. His death carried with it all the sin and suffering of the world. If the story had ended there it would be one of tragedy and defeat. It would have been a heroic but futile gesture alongside many thousands of others. The 'suffering servant' would be an embarrassment.

But the story does not end there. The resurrection is essential to the Christian faith; in it, God authenticates humanity and the life of the body. Yet the humanity represented by the risen Christ is not the old humanity, but a person who has defeated sin and death. We look for signs of what that means for us and our identity; in the words of disabled theologian Nancy Eiesland, 'this is the disabled God'. Eiesland reflected on what God would look like if God was to identify with her experience. She says that she waited 'for a mighty revelation of God'.

> But my epiphany bore little resemblance to the God I was expect-
> ing or the God of my dreams. I saw God in a sip-puff wheelchair,
> that is the chair used most often by quadriplegics enabling them
> to manoeuvre by blowing and sucking on a strawlike device.
> Not an omnipotent self-sufficient God, but neither a pitiable
> suffering servant. In this moment, I beheld God as a survivor,
> unpitying and forthright. I recognized the incarnate Christ in
> the image of those judged 'not feasible,' 'unemployable,' with
> 'questionable quality of life.' Here was God for me.[6]

For Eiesland, it is the continuity between this person and the risen Christ that is important. The risen Christ still has the marks of the crucifixion in his body (John 20.19–29). Indeed, these unique distinguishing marks are required to convince even those who knew him well that he is who he says he is. When he first appears to the disciples he shows them his wounds and they believe. On a second occasion, when Thomas is present having been missing the first time, Jesus explicitly invites him to explore his wounds as the key to his identity. Nancy Eiesland says of this:

In presenting his impaired hands and feet to his startled friends, the resurrected Jesus is revealed as the disabled God. Jesus, the resurrected Savior, calls for his frightened companions to recognize in the marks of impairment their own connection with God, their own salvation. In so doing, this disabled God is also the revealer of a new humanity. The disabled God is not only the one from heaven but the revelation of true personhood, underscoring the reality that full personhood is fully compatible with the experience of disability.[7]

So we do not have to be 'normalized' in order to celebrate our 'true personhood'. A disabled person can shout in celebration, with the psalmist, 'I praise you because I am fearfully and wonderfully made' (Ps. 139.14). The disabled God shows us that if we try to form a Church that worships a hero without wounds we ignore what the Church is for. Paul says that knowing Christ involves experiencing both power and suffering when he says, 'I want to know Christ – yes, to know the power of his resurrection and participation in his sufferings' (Phil. 3.10).

Christians look forward to a New World that, we are promised, will be without sin, death or suffering. Yet the vision of that New World opens up as many questions as it resolves. Does it have implications for the lives of disabled people as they are lived now? In what sense will our bodies be transformed? We long for a transformed world in which justice will be done and oppressed people liberated, but some are hesitant. Does that world favour some and not others? Will there be winners and losers in the New World? It is to this fourth theme that we now turn.

7

Completion

———◆◆◆———

Ask anyone where they aspire to be in ten years' time, and you will learn a lot about their desires, priorities, self-esteem and expectations of life. You will gain an insight into their character. Some may desire a life of selfless service; others will want to achieve ambitions of accumulating wealth or high status. But there will be some who, lacking any hope for the future, will see no prospect of changing what they view as their hopeless situation.

Our identity is as shaped by what we long for as by what we have experienced – where we are going as much as where we have come from. We are created by God with meaning and purpose, but that is not enough to shape our identity; we also need to know where we are heading. Our identity depends on our destiny. We live in the light of the future as much as we build on the experience of the past.

In describing human identity we nearly always start with the portrayal of the image of God in Genesis 1—2, as we have done earlier in this book. But to gain an idea of the significance of humanity we must know not only its origins but its destiny. It is this that marks out the Christian world-view as distinctive. Other religions may share the vision of the image of God in Genesis. Secular perspectives may also have a high view of the individual which bestows on humanity both dignity and rights.

But Christianity has a vision that is based on an event that has already happened in history: the resurrection of Jesus Christ. The New World that Christianity looks forward to is guaranteed by the resurrection of Jesus; he has defeated sin and death, opening up the door to that world. The portrayal of the future of humanity based on that vision is not only distinctive, it is unique. It cannot be shared by any other creed or belief system since only those who believe in the resurrection and its fundamental significance for our lives have any interest in it. If we didn't believe, the idea of the resurrection would be nonsensical and the idea of a New World based on it fanciful.

So, in discussing human identity we can start as readily from the specifics of the New World as from the creation narrative in Genesis 1—2. Indeed, there is an added bonus to working backwards. When we work with a creation ethic we develop a world-view that is applicable to all humanity. The idea of the image of God is applicable to all human beings whether they have religious beliefs or not. This is essential for any theological reflection on issues such as human rights, the nature of work, marriage and sexuality, or environmental ethics. However, if we want to develop a world-view that is uniquely Christian, we can start with the nature of the New World, and what kind of people we will be in order to live in that world.

There is a second virtue to this approach, in that it is Christological. Any anthropology that is Christian has to be viewed through the lens that is Jesus Christ. We are told that he 'is the image of the invisible God' (Col. 1.15) and that the world was made by him and for him (John 1.3). We also learn that we 'shall be like him' (1 John 3.2) in that we will all individually and diversely reflect who Jesus is.

Our biblical timeline is now fastened at both ends. Creation, compromise and covenant have now resulted in completion. The purposes set in motion by God at the creation of this world are now completed in the creation of the New World. Theologian Stanley Grenz says of this:

> In one sense, creation is an event in the primordial past. In another sense, however, creation is not a past but a future event. The creation of the world does not merely begin the temporal sequence. More significantly, it stands at the end of the historical

process. 'Creation' indicates God's future completion of his work in bringing the universe to its destined state. It is his act in making the world in accordance with the divine design. Viewed in this manner, the act of creation is not yet completed, for God is active in history bringing about his world-creating work.[1]

Our awareness that completion lies in the future gives us our first insight into our current condition, which is that we are *unfinished*. We are provisional in the bodies we have, the experiences we go through and the communities we live in. This should not be confused with the idea that we are sinful. It is simply saying that nothing we experience in this life, from the nature of our bodies to the experiences we call 'spiritual', should be thought of as normative. As the apostle Paul says, 'we see through a glass, darkly' (1 Cor. 13.12, AV). No aspect of our lives can be said to have reached completion, and that is true universally. No one, however rich or beautiful, can set themselves up as the norm in comparison to which the rest of us feel inadequate.

Our bodies break down as we age, succumb to illness or live with impairments. Our relationships, always fragile, may break down and cause us pain. Our institutions disappoint us, no longer leading us in the ways of justice. In every direction we look we find that this life is provisional – we are unfinished. But we know that only because we are sure that something better is coming: the day of completion. That is what it means to live in hope.

The three themes that have run through this book so far, as we have looked at the nature of humanity, are the personal, the relational and the social. We now look at how these three are affected by the biblical theme of *completion*.

Transformed people

The Bible tells us that we are complete in Christ (Col. 2.10), yet Christ lived an unfinished life, as we do. He was not sinful but he was unfinished. That is what it meant for him to give up the glory of heaven, as Paul tells us in Philippians, and take on the form of a servant (Phil. 2.7). Here was a man who experienced joy and love but who was hungry, suffered and was tempted, as we are. He was 'fully man and fully God', which means that we can look at his life and ask how we too can live an unfinished life that is honouring to God. For those grappling with disability theology, it is important to recognize that although the unfinished life is the norm in that we all live it, it is not normative in that it is not an expression of the fullness of what it means to be human. It is the norm in that even Jesus had to live it; there is no other kind of human life. But it is not normative as it is not our destiny. What is normative is the New World, and it is that to which we aspire.

People sometimes ask me, 'What kind of person will I be in the New World?' They have got as far as accepting that there is a New World to come ('the new heavens and the new earth'), as opposed to belief in an ephemeral concept of 'heaven', but been unable to get any further. It is natural to be intrigued by what the New World will be like, and what kind of people we will be as a result. There are two perspectives to come to terms with here.

The first perspective sees no reason for disabled people to be changed in order to be members of any 'New World'. Since having an impairment is about diversity rather than deficiency there is nothing to be changed. Disabled people take their place among the multitudes worshipping together. Such a perspective sees the conventional view of the New World as the ultimate expression of the medical model of disability. As in Christian healing where some see the issue as normalizing the body (turning the disabled body into one that is not), so the conventional idea of the New World is the most blatant manifestation of the need for being normalized in order to be acceptable.

However, it is possible to *over-identify* with our impairments as being a necessary expression of our identity. For some, having their impairment removed in the New World means that they are being rejected in this world. But what other parts of our current identity are we to hold on to in case their disappearance in the New World is also a sign that we are being rejected now? It is all very well to have a vision of the streets of the New World having ramps everywhere but I don't see that living in a 'New World' with my impaired brain and the possibility that I will have a seizure at any moment is anything to write home about. Those who see the New World only as a place for the acceptance of disabled people such as myself and not for the transformation of our lives do have to come to terms with the fact that some impairments include, as part of the package deal, immense pain, terror and confusion. Yet if the New World is anything, it is a place without suffering. We cannot pick and choose impairments that we want to include unchanged in the New World as a living metaphor of the equality of disabled and abled people, without seeming to judge those who long to be relieved of the burden of their impairment and look with hope for a New World coming.

What this view is quite rightly seeking to avoid is the perspective that the New World is a place where all that is *normal* is blessed. As I have already mentioned, there is a view held by many Christians that the New World is a place where those of us who are deemed normal are let in with few changes being necessary, but where disabled people will be radically transformed. It is this view that is being rejected by those who want to see the New World as affirming disabled people rather than changing them. Not only is it fundamentally judgemental in that abled people are holding themselves up as the standard by which others should be judged, but it is apparently ignorant of the extent to which we all need to be changed in the New World. It is also a sign that abled people do not recognize just how much of their view of themselves as 'normal' is due to this world discriminating in their favour.

After all, what is normal in the New World is not apparent now. Just as Christ still has the wounds in his hands in the New

World, so we may still carry the hallmarks of our impairments but their significance will be transformed. Those who think of the New World as a place for 'normal' people need to think again. In fact this transformed community may be the very place where some people we have called 'disabled' find that some of the characteristics that society saw as marking them out as disabled remain in the New World. What has happened is that the community has changed so that those characteristics are no longer seen as 'a problem' but can be celebrated in the New World.

The second perspective is built on the strong theme running through the Bible that the New World is a place where disabled people no longer have to live with the activity limitations and participation restrictions that are currently a part of their daily lives. Isaiah talks of a place and a time where the lame leap, mute speak, deaf hear and blind see (Isa. 35.6). For those who view this as the place where they truly belong and the people they are meant to be, impairment is one factor that prevents them from being free to be themselves. Far from it being the New World that is a place of alienation, it turns out that it is this world in which we struggle together to become the people we want to be. Here is the ultimate goal to which the healings of Jesus pointed. He healed a few in order to show that the New World existed and what kind of place it would be. Yet he did not just heal disabled people in order to show that. He called for the transformation and reorientation of all people if they were to enter into 'the kingdom of God'. He was trying to tell us something fundamental about our human identity.

We cannot be reduced to the performance of our body, its shape or capacity. Christians believe that there is more to people 'than meets the eye'. Our past, present and future identities are integrated with the physical, emotional and spiritual expressions of who we are. What we see of each other and what we know of ourselves is only a very small part of who we are. Compared to who God knows me to be, my self-knowledge is minuscule. My feelings about myself change, as do my memories of what I have done and the stories I tell about myself. Earlier we saw that to be made in the image of God is to be in relationship with God. Here we can go further in seeing what that means. It is to trust that God relates to the totality of who we are and not who I suppose myself to be on any given morning. That is why the idea that God loves us and wants the best for us is overwhelming, since God lives with the whole me not the Monday-morning me.

At the heart of this insight is the concept of trust. God lives with the totality of who I am, a small part of which is the person I know myself to be today or the part of me that is my impairment; can't I trust God to do the best by me in a New World that (I am told) is prepared for those who love him? To equate ourselves with our impairments is surely to over-identify with them. We should not be victims because of them, nor should we ignore them in a kind of false heroism but see them as something we live with for now. From the standpoint of the New World, we are temporarily disabled people.

The apostle Paul was certainly asked the question, 'What kind of bodies will we have when we die?' In 1 Corinthians 15 he gives his answer. Essentially, he says two things. First, he sees our current bodies as inadequate. They are 'perishable' and 'mortal'. This applies to all human beings. Instead he says we shall one day have 'imperishable' and 'immortal' bodies. Second, he says that we shall *all* be transformed. This is not a community where there is a standard set by normal people while others are 'brought up to scratch'. This is a universal judgement on the state of our bodies. We are *all* in need of transformation. That is a humbling thought but is, as so often in the Bible, sharply realistic. It is not a case of whether we will recognize our friends who have impairments in 'heaven'. That is the ultimate in discrimination as it suggests that we do not need to change, but that they do. No. We will all be changed.

Some have seen in this the ultimate redemption of the medical model of disability. After all, Paul is stating that there is something wrong about the body. But this is a universal comment. It applies to the whole human race, not to a particular group within it. Paul is not comparing us to one another and finding one group wanting. He is comparing our current bodies with the ones we will have (or need) to participate in the New World. He does not differentiate in any way between abled and disabled people in this world.

To be transformed in this way is not one of rejection but of *preparation*. It is necessary for us to be different in order to experience the New World. Our old bodies could not cope with its demands nor delight in its pleasures. If we were to keep our old bodies in the New World it would be like walking through a perfumed garden with no sense of smell or sitting alone with no stamina while others explore the highest mountains with ease or swim against the tide in the strongest seas.

Renewed relationships

We have noted already that the basic building block of human identity is not the autonomous individual but the *person in relationship*. Individuals can live in fragmented and atomistic societies but people live in relationship and form communities. So just as we have asked, 'What kind of body will I have in the New World?', it is important to ask 'What kind of relationships will I have in the New World?'

The response, the one that was given by Jesus to this question, is that he saw his family as going beyond his biological family. In the New World was a promise to everyone that they would share in the intimacy that he had enjoyed in his family life:

> Now Jesus' mother and brothers came to see him, but they were not able to get near him because of the crowd. Someone told him, 'Your mother and brothers are standing outside, wanting to see you.' He replied, 'My mother and brothers are those who hear God's word and put it into practice.' (Luke 8.19–21)

When Jesus was faced with a scenario that involved a question about relationships in the New World, he had this to say:

> That same day the Sadducees, who say there is no resurrection, came to him with a question. 'Teacher,' they said, 'Moses told us that if a man dies without having children, his brother must marry the widow and raise up offspring for him. Now there were seven brothers among us. The first one married and died, and since he had no children, he left his wife to his brother. The same thing happened to the second and third brother, right on down to the seventh. Finally, the woman died. Now then, at the resurrection, whose wife will she be of the seven, since all of them were married to her?' Jesus replied, 'You are in error because you do not know the Scriptures or the power of God. At the resurrection people will neither marry nor be given in marriage; they will be like the angels in heaven. But about the resurrection of the dead – have you not read what God said to you, "I am the God of Abraham, the God of Isaac, and the God of Jacob"? He is not the God of the dead but of the living.' (Matt. 22.23–32)

Often comments about this passage assume that Jesus is saying that there is no sex in heaven, and have seen this as a negative. In fact, Jesus is saying that there will be much more than we currently experience, in the intimacy of marriage or in any other relationship in this world. Just as it is inappropriate to regret the loss of our impairments because we look forward to the transformation of our bodies, so it is inappropriate to mourn relationships, which will be transformed in ways we cannot currently imagine.

Paul does not describe the kind of body we shall have in the New World; and on the question of relationships Jesus is similarly unspecific, saying only that we shall be 'like the angels'. There is a good reason for that. If we were to discover the kind of body that flourishes in the New World, or know in advance exactly what our relationships will be like, this would disadvantage those whose bodies are furthest from this eschatological ideal, and they may find themselves oppressed by those who most closely resemble it. On occasion a free society operates best when its citizens are ignorant of certain things. The Bible is wisely silent on many issues.

The New Society

The third theme in our discussion of what it means to be complete is that of community. There are many pictures of the New Society: the multitude in front of the throne; the City of God, which descends to earth accompanied by the voice saying, 'God's dwelling place is now among the people' (Rev. 21.3).

From the standpoint of disability, the New World is one of full *participation*. This goes beyond the usual discussion of accessibility to a community designed and run by others. This is a picture of equal participation in the community.

The New World is also about *liberation*. In this society it is impossible to displease God. Evil has been not only defeated but done away with. Liberation comes not because God restricts our activity to that which pleases him, but because we are free at last. There are no choices to be made that are bad choices. This has been the goal of history – that by their own choice people should be truly free. This is a place without stigma, suffering, tragedy and disaster. This is liberation with participation.

Last, this New World is marked by *exploration*. Just as the first creation was an unprecedented explosion of God's imagination, so too the New World will be an extraordinary witness to God's fertile mind. As Paul says, 'What no eye has seen, what no ear has heard, and what no mind has conceived – these things God has prepared for those who love him' (1 Cor. 2.9).

In the last book of the Narnia chronicles by C. S. Lewis,[2] the children with Aslan the Lion (representing Christ) defeat the evil army of Tash. They find themselves liberated from the cares of this world, invited by Aslan to participate in the world he has prepared for them and to explore it endlessly. As he bounds ahead of them he roars, 'Further up and further in'. This is a world without barriers.

8

Healing and cure

————•◦•————

We have explored four of the key themes of the Christian faith. It is now time to look at two pressing issues with respect to disability and theology. The first is attitudes to healing, the second is the consequences for the Church if it is to take disability seriously. In both areas there is enormous potential for the lives of disabled people to be celebrated and affirmed. There is also potential for exclusion and damage.

A key issue we have to face when we come to the sensitive subject of healing is that we do not approach it neutrally. We each have expectations of what healing is and what it does. Indeed, while we may not express our views formally there is an instinct in each of us as to what can happen in the world, as we understand it. For everyone there are phenomena that lie beyond the bounds of belief and about which we remain to be convinced. This is partly due to personal experience. One person may have frequently been present at healings so he can speak about them with familiarity; the person he is talking to may never have witnessed anything similar, and she struggles to comprehend what he is talking about, or even doubts that what is being claimed has actually happened. Sometimes modern medicine provides an alternative story. A person may get out of her wheelchair and walk after many years of being incapacitated, but according to doctors there may be a perfectly good medical explanation for how this can happen. We have separated modern medicine from divine gift, so we feel that the one displaces the other.

In the modern world we have in-built expectations of how things work, usually in terms of cause and effect. We turn a key and the car engine starts. We press a switch and the light comes on. In terms of mechanics we are steeped in the scientific world-view. The knowledge derived from it has brought us great power and that power has given us the ability to control our lives. Science is generated by the power of theory, at the heart of which is a logic that provides a coherent and consistent explanation of what is happening, and a prediction of what will happen when certain conditions are met. But theory is not the same as theology. At the heart of theology there is a mystery – the nature of God. Attempting to reduce theology to theory by asking how healing 'works' is to rob theology of its heart, which is the freedom of God in Christ.

Healing is inextricably related to prayer. The very fact that we ask for something means that we have an expectation that an answer may be given. That in turn presupposes that we believe that the world may change in answer to our prayers. To pray that someone be healed is one of those prayers. Of course, some people are of the opinion that the purpose of prayer is not to change the world but to change us, to bring our will into line with that of God. While that is true – prayer is definitely set on discerning God's will both for us and for our prayers – the New Testament also encourages us to pray for the healing of others; and unless we think that this applied only in some age long gone, we are invited to do the same now.

Prayer is an indication that we believe that God is present with us, and that God's presence is the focus of all that we do and the fulcrum about which our behaviour turns. What we say and how we behave is dictated by our understanding of who God is and how God works. But when God is present, so is mystery, because God acts according to his own freedom. Theologian Karl Barth once said that God 'loves in freedom'.[1] We may feel frustration in wanting to see people healed, but God shows himself on his own terms and timetable, not on ours.

When and where God heals is not a problem that needs to be solved. To approach healing in that way would be to have a very distorted view of it. It would be to assume that healing belongs to the modern world of cause and effect in which we live. The power and significance of God has given way, over the last few hundred years, to the ability of humanity to determine its own destiny. Divine providence has been replaced by individual freedom of choice. We are led to believe that society is at its most powerful when life is reduced to techniques over which we have complete control. Correspondingly, we are at our most powerless when something we desperately want to happen remains outside our grasp. Like oil and water, mystery and technique cannot be mixed.

We are used to getting our own way. We want results when we pray for somebody, immediately. We are creatures of Western culture living in the eternal present. But God lives with our story past, present and future, and the actions of this free and loving God can be understood only when that whole story is revealed. The snap judgements we make about what God has done (or has not done) fall far short of the ultimate unveiling of the story of our lives. Perhaps we do not see the unintentional consequences of our actions or our own desires. We may judge that a person's impairment is a result of God's displeasure, whereas their life may be full of blessing. We are myopic, and this is one reason why it is good to remain humble about what we claim.

Countless attempts have been made in the area of healing to find an effective technique that will bring about the desired results. This should come as no surprise to us, given the nature of our society. High-profile claims that some technique will 'work' in bringing about effective healings come and go with rapidity, as does the celebrity status of those who promote them. In an area of life that depends so much on the mystery of the freedom of God, the failure of a technique can only leave a trail of disillusioned people in its wake.

Even though we cannot explain mystery, because it belongs to the freedom of God's love, we can try to understand why something might have to remain a mystery. For example, if healing could be reduced to a technique it would confer power on those who knew how to manipulate it. Eventually the technique itself would displace the necessity for God to be the priority in healing prayer. We would not need to 'practise the presence of God'; we would be left not with grateful thanks for what God has done but pride in what we can accomplish. This should remind us of the tower of Babel, where people tried by their own efforts to increase their own status at the expense of God's sovereignty. The disastrous ending to that story should be warning enough that to pretend that our preferred outcomes are shared by God is not only foolhardy but idolatrous.

Whatever happens when we pray needs to be placed in the context of salvation. The God to whom we pray is the God who loves us and desires the best for us. Even if we continue to suffer and do not experience a cure, we still live before a God who loves us and who is present with us. When we pray, we seek Christ first and we do so unconditionally. We desire to be the person God wants us to be today and to be prepared by the Holy Spirit for the person we are to be tomorrow. We cannot know what that person will be. We may be involved in an accident of some kind and find ourselves with permanent and substantial impairments as a result. What we should not do is see the power of the risen Christ as the means to an end, and if that end does not materialize be led to doubt God.[2] In short, we should not 'compartmentalize' healing, viewing it as separate from the claims of the gospel in our lives; nor should we see Christ just as a source of power for our own healing. If there is any wisdom to be found about the mystery of healing, we will understand it only by reflecting on its place in the story of redemption inspired by the grace of God.

So we do the worst thing possible if we convince somebody who is in need that healing prayer belongs to the realm of cause and effect, and that if he 'believes enough' he will be healed. In all prayer we strike a balance between knowing that God will keep his promises and yet will act according to his own freedom. In other words we hand over control to God, and we need to make that plain to anyone we are praying for or with.

In this regard the best context for healing prayer is the local church, where those who are experienced in prayer, 'the elders of the church' (according to James 5.14), can pray for those whose character and story they know intimately. They will be familiar with those who come forward for prayer, and are themselves well known, concerned with maintaining their integrity and reputation. In short, there is mutual accountability, which is both healthy and wise. This is in contrast with the anonymous and highly charged public meeting where a visiting celebrity healer comes and goes without accountability or any relationship with the person being prayed for – this would be perhaps the worst context. But in the local church the remarkable can blend with the ordinary, and both can be accommodated into the uncomfortable demands of mutual respect and love that characterize the body of Christ. Such a mix provides an encouragement that God is listening to the prayers of ordinary people as they go about their day-to-day business. It also inspires us to look for God in the everyday and be sensitive to the presence of healing (or the need for it) in our relationships with others. Our delight in seeing God in the ordinary may then temper our inordinate desire to see God always in the extraordinary.

However, if the local church is to be a place of affirmation and joy it needs to be honest about healing. Accountability extends not just to the leadership of the church but to every member. I remember once being in a church when a man who had one leg shorter than the other and walked with a pronounced limp went up to the front and, in tears, told the congregation that God had healed him. His legs were now both the same length and he no longer walked with a limp. Then, accompanied by deathly silence in the church, he limped back to his seat. Did anyone challenge him? Not to my knowledge. When dubious assertions are made about healings witnessed or prophecies fulfilled it can be difficult to be honest in response; but the Church claims to be founded on truth, and we must become involved in the uncomfortable because love and respect require it.

Jesus and healing

Luke tells us that Jesus healed a man who was demon-possessed (Luke 8.35). The man lived among the tombs, naked, and restrained by the chains that were an attempt by his former neighbours to control him. After Jesus had healed him we are told that he sat at the feet of Jesus, 'dressed and in his right mind'. The miracle is extraordinary, but who provided the clothes? Who unlocked the chains? They signify his re-entry into society – a familiar result of the healing miracles of Jesus. Leaving the man naked would have been only half the story. Someone else completed the healing of Jesus by providing the clothes and unlocking the chains.

All the healings of Jesus were statements of the 'already' and the 'not yet' of the kingdom of God. Each was in some sense partial in that they pointed to a greater salvation that could be embraced only by those who entered the kingdom of God. Every healing, though enjoyed in the present, pointed forward to the New World where each of us will be transformed. Jesus is in fact saying, 'Here is a down-payment of what the kingdom of God will be like when it is fully realized.' There was a direct link between the good that Jesus was doing and the goal towards which it pointed. But both the method he used and the goal (immediate *and* ultimate) had to be good for it to be in accordance with the kingdom of God.

Through his healing ministry, Jesus drew attention to the embodied spirituality of each person. Forgiveness often accompanied healing, which should not surprise us: the word for 'healing' in the Greek is the same as that for 'salvation' (*soteria*). In other words, there is always something beyond Jesus' miraculous cures. They are acts of love, restoration and reconciliation. And they are acts in which we have a part to play, as did the person who provided the clothes for the man who found himself sane but naked.

Every act of healing has consequences for the culture in which it takes place. Jesus challenged the authorities on the subject of whether or not it was lawful to heal on the Sabbath. When no answer was forthcoming he healed the man anyway. The authorities had lost a sense of the meaning of the Sabbath. They were bound up with the regulations that smothered its real purpose, and had forgotten what that was. By healing, Jesus was acting in accordance with the real nature of the Sabbath, demonstrating its true meaning.

When Jesus healed people some, if not all, of the following happened.

- They had a greater sense of well-being.
- They no longer suffered.
- They praised God.
- They were embraced rather than avoided.
- They had a higher social status than before.
- They heard the good news of the kingdom.
- They were restored to family and friends.
- They had a new place in the community.
- They had the possibility of gaining employment.
- They were invited to become a disciple.
- They were given food or clothed.

Of course, this does not all happen explicitly in the case of each person Jesus heals, but it is often implied. Consider the stigma attached to disability and illness in a society where sin and sickness were viewed as being linked. Healing removed that stigma automatically, changing a person's social status, place in the community and access to employment. Healing meant that a leper, for instance, could be touched or experience intimacy, perhaps for the first time in years.

Healing and cure

So what should we expect when we pray for healing? As we have seen, we often desire a cure expressed as a particular outcome. Yet if the only thing we will regard as 'success' as a result of our prayer is the physical cure of the person before us, we are on shaky ground. We have set the criteria for success and failure. If nothing happens, then an explanation is necessary; and since God cannot be found wanting, it is usually those prayed for who feel that it is somehow their fault that nothing has happened.

The pitfalls that await us when we pray for a cure to be the sign that healing has taken place can be avoided but we must radically amend our way of thinking. Of course, we have to reject any perspective that claims that God cannot physically cure people today. To do so would be to deny the numerous stories of people who have witnessed such events, and to call into question whether God can intervene in the world in any sense. All that is necessary is to reverse our expectations. Everything falls into place if we believe that healing is the rule and cure is the exception. When we do this we will be drawn into the extraordinary depths of what constitutes healing in the Christian Church.

Some people are cured as a result of prayer – and that is something that needs to be celebrated. But many others have been prayed for on countless occasions without any visible result. Disabled people may feel, as some have said to me, that the attitude towards them is that 'next time you might be lucky'. Some no longer go to church because they have the impression that they are viewed as an object to be healed rather than a person to be loved. Nevertheless, best practice should be celebrated. We lovingly and sincerely pray for them, laying hands on them or anointing them with oil. This is no mean thing. We are mandated to do it in the New Testament, and it should not be looked down upon. But in praying for healing, if we are now to separate this from the physical cure, we must expect to become involved in more than the prayer alone. For instance, we should examine the extent to which healing is a social phenomenon into which we are all drawn. To what extent is healing about 'well-being'? Just as in baptism, when a person is baptized into the body of Christ and welcomed by his church by a public affirmation, so the prayer for healing is an opportunity for such affirmation and a drawing into the love and acceptance of the Church.

We have already discussed how our own identity is both personal and social, and how we are affected by the way others relate to us. This can be most evident in the delicate circumstances where someone requests prayer. The grace and love with which they are treated, the respect for them as a person, the echo of God's unconditional love for them, are all essential parts of the salvation message that is the very bedrock of our attitude to them at that moment of vulnerability. That moment is a shared memory and all involved contribute to it.

Praying for healing is also a prayer for the healing of the Church. When someone with permanent and substantial impairments is prayed for but is not physically changed in any way, that church has to face up to the situation. We see the possibility of prayer as a way to a cure, but for the moment, it seems, this has not 'worked'. Several things have changed, though. First, the individuals return to their seats bearing the load of seemingly unanswered prayer. Will others talk to them about this, or will it be ignored? Ignoring what has happened may make it seem as if it is the fault of those being prayed for. The question is, if we love them, how do we express that love when such prayer has apparently gone unanswered? Second, while they may have needs, as we all do, they will also have gifts, which may have been overlooked by the church because the emphasis has been on them as people in need of a cure. Are they always to be prayed for, or could they be members of the prayer team too? Third, are they being treated as if they have lives outside the church? Everyone, whether disabled or not, has multiple needs, and the church should remember this. There may be carers who need support. If a church does not feel that it has any responsibility to people beyond the mandates of institutional religion, then can it be said to be a 'healing community' – even if fervent prayers are offered on a regular basis for people to be cured? One person may pray for a cure, but healing is a matter for the whole Christian community.

Indeed, the question we need to ask is, 'Have the individuals who have been prayed for been blessed or wounded by their experience?' Healing prayer accompanied by affirmation, love and solidarity can send people back to their seats feeling happy and confident that they did the right thing in going forward. But it is possible to pray for them in such a way that they feel uncomfortable and look for the exit. There is a world of difference between the 'wounded healer', whose gentleness comes from personal experience of suffering, and the 'unhealed wounder', who projects an internal trauma on to those with whom he or she associates.[3] Churches need a great deal of wisdom in discerning who should pray for their church family, since a mistake can cause distress for many. In her book *Resilient Pastors*, Justine Allain-Chapman looks at the concept of the 'wounded healer' made popular by Henri Nouwen,[4] and concludes that it can sometimes focus too much on being wounded and not enough about healing. Her call is for 'resilience'. A pastor may have been wounded but the issue is whether he or she is resilient: 'Once pastors are self-aware enough to recognize their own woundedness they need to attend to their wounds so that they may be of service to others, otherwise they cause damage.'[5]

It is easy for a pastor to try to lead his congregation by telling them that he shares their wounds, thinking that this will lead to their healing. But it does not. What they need is a leader who *has been* wounded but who has come through the experience with resilience. It is resilience that people associate with healing, not staying with one's wounds. If the leader is still in a state of woundedness, how can he lead the people to a place of healing? If he is walking in darkness then whatever his qualifications, or the size of his church, he needs to be ministered to himself, instead of perhaps being someone who staggers on alone, bearing the load, seeing ministry as autonomy, trying to hide his misery. Henri Nouwen is right to point out that love and sensitivity can come from a person who has been wounded, but this should be balanced by the need of the church to be led by one who can bring them into an experience of joy, healing and liberation.

We read in the New Testament that the healings of Jesus led people to another place from the one they associated with their 'wounds'. The Gospel accounts indicate that many of Jesus' healings enabled people to rejoin their community or their families. Some, such as lepers, had been outcasts, and forced by their circumstances to beg. Many could now be welcomed back into their families. Others decided to become disciples of Jesus and left their former lives. The parallel question relating to our prayers for the healing of others today is whether we are willing to become engaged in the same consequences. Would we offer to find clothes for the man who was a demoniac, or go for the key to unlock his chains? What are we prepared to do beyond offering the prayer itself? It can be a feature of the 'celebrity' healing ministry that those who operate at these extremes are interested only in cure, and that as a form of entertainment. All too often disabled people tell of experiences at healing meetings where the person 'with the gift of healing' was not interested in them once it became evident that they had not been 'cured'. They may then have been bundled off the stage to make way for the next candidate. Spurious claims are also sometimes made; Professor John Hull, for example, who is blind, relates how it was pronounced that he had been healed when he had not.[6] Disability theologian Nancy Eiesland says:

> Resurrection is not about the negation or erasure of our disabled bodies in hopes of perfect images, untouched by physical disability; rather Christ's resurrection offers hope that our nonconventional, and sometimes difficult, bodies participate fully in the imago Dei and that God whose nature is love and who is on the side of justice and solidarity is touched by our experience. God is changed by the experience of being a disabled body. This is what the Christian hope of resurrection means.[7]

The significance of the resurrection is not that Jesus is obliged to offer us a cure, otherwise the power of the resurrection is called into question. The resurrection is the greatest demonstration of life-transforming power in human history. Compared to that, what is a mere cure for our own impairments? But he still bears the marks of the crucifixion. He offers salvation to all, but his body, in showing how he suffered, offers solidarity with all those who remain disabled. He has taken up the marks of disability into himself and has transformed their significance for ever. The idea of the resurrection meaning that everyone should now be cured is a disastrous one. From her own perspective, Nancy Eiesland, far from being negative, provides a balance between the all too frequent negative experience of curing disabled people and a wonderfully positive one.

> My own history with laying on of hands has been an ambiguous one. Often the practice has been closely associated with ritual healing. I, like many disabled people, have experienced the negative effects of healing rituals. Healing has been the churchly parallel to rehabilitative medicine, in which the goal was

'normalization' of the bodies of disabled people . . . Yet I have also experienced laying on of hands that was restorative and redemptive. These physical mediations of God's grace have often kept me related to my body at times when all of my impulses pushed me toward dissociating from the pain-racked, uncomfortable beast. For example, as a child after spending several months in hospitals having my body rebuilt surgically, I was a participant in a powerful service of laying on of hands. In a charismatic meeting in a rural North Dakota parish, I experienced the body care of several elderly nuns schooled in physical attendance as nurses and touched by the spirit as Christians. Their touch and tears were the body practices of inclusion. My body belonged in the church. From that early age, I recall the physical sensation of having my body redeemed for God as those spiritual women laid hands on me, caressing my pain, lifting my isolation, and revealing my spiritual body. For disabled people, such experiences of physical redemption and ordinary inclusion are rare.[8]

If this is the God who offers solidarity with those society calls disabled, and who sees communion and vulnerability as hallmarks of all human life, then this has profound implications not only for how we see disability but for how we answer the question, 'Who am I?'

There are also profound implications for the healing ministry of the Church. At present the Church's view of disability is very much along the lines of the medical model. A body is deficient in that it deviates from perceived social norms. Healing, as seemingly authenticated by the ministry of Jesus, aims to restore the functioning of the body to those norms. To put it bluntly, healing should change a person who is disabled into a person who is not. But because Jesus rose with the marks of suffering still on him, disability implies not a deficient body but a fully human body.

Haydon Spenceley, an ordinand in the Church of England, is a wheelchair user who lives with cerebral palsy. He says:

All of us need healing. I certainly do. I would say that I have been healed many times. Certainly, my perception of myself, who God is, who other people are, and how we all relate to one another, particularly in my relation to my having cerebral palsy, has been healed and is constantly being healed. Do I need to be able to walk? No. Do I need to accept the offer of salvation, freedom and hope that Christ offers to me, and to all? Most certainly. God creating me as an impaired person is a blessing, not a curse. I am not sick. I am impaired. Sometimes disabled people are healed physically, sometimes emotionally or spiritually. More often than not, though, it is a healing of relationships which needs to take place. There needs to be healing in the relationship between God and his people, and in the relationship between his Church and those who are currently outside it . . . We don't need to be physically, mentally or emotionally perfect before we're allowed in.[9]

Do you need to be cured in order to be healed? The answer is a resounding no! It's a possibility, perhaps even a desirability. But healing is on offer to all who want it, as Haydon points out. To be healed is to enter into salvation. You may be blind or deaf, or live with epilepsy or multiple sclerosis, but have entered into an experience of healing that has liberated you, made you aware of God's love and energized you to fight for others. My mother lived with intolerable head pain for over 20 years, but for those who met her she was a woman of faith whose loving presence was a healing one.

And it is possible to be cured, but not healed. This is illustrated by the story of the ten lepers in Luke 17.12–19. Ten lepers cry out to Jesus to have mercy on them. In effect they are asking him to rid them of their leprosy. He tells them to go to the priest to be cleansed, which was the appropriate practice, as the priest had to certify them as free from disease. On their way, their leprosy miraculously disappeared. But only one returned to thank Jesus and to praise God. In the story this person was, ironic-ally, a Samaritan; that is, he belonged to a community loathed by the Jewish people. This man received much more than a cure of his leprosy. He praised God for what had happened to him, his faith was affirmed by Jesus, he discovered a love that transcended ethnic tensions; he threw himself at the feet of Jesus, expressing his gratitude. This man was both cured and healed. He entered into a relationship with God that day. He rose to his feet as a new man both physically and spiritually. The story is rightly about him. Where the others went we have no idea.

So if a cure is on offer, do we take it? Nancy Mairs, a writer who lives with multiple sclerosis, recognizes the need to be realistic in facing up to having an impairment:

> All the same, if a cure were found, would I take it? In a minute. I may be a cripple, but I'm only occasionally a loony and never a saint. Anyway in my brand of theology God doesn't give bonus points for a limp. I'd take a cure. I just don't need one. A friend who also has MS startled me once by asking, 'Do you ever say to yourself, "Why me Lord?"' 'No Michael, I don't,' I told him, 'because whenever I try, the only response I can think of is, "Why not?"' If I could make a cosmic deal, who would I put in my place? What in my life would I give up in exchange for sound limbs and a thrilling rush of energy? No one. Nothing. I might as well do the job myself. Now that I'm getting the hang of it.[10]

The problem is that many people, when they see a person with an overt impairment, assume that what that person wants more than anything is a cure.

Haydon Spenceley recently had an experience that illustrates this. In a blog called 'Please Stop Pretending I'm Not Human', he describes what happened.

> 'Good morning, sir. May the Lord God grant you the healing that you need. Amen.'
> I had an interaction this morning, of which this was the sum total. As I was pushing along towards Abington Street in Northampton, a man walked towards me, said those words, hit me on the shoulder and carried on walking. He did not look back. I know. I checked.

This isn't the first time this has happened to me in my life (I figure I must need an awful lot of healing, but then don't we all), but today, in the light of a lot of things that have happened in the last couple of years, the camel's back has been broken by the straw.

After looking at the implications of this in detail he concludes:

What's broken in me? Is it my lack of ability to walk? I don't think so (you might have guessed that by now). So let's do a deal, ok? Next time you walk past me in the street, if you feel led to pray for me to be healed, think again. If you still feel the need to pray for me to be healed, be ready for me to do the same to you, and be aware that I'm asking for a lot more than just to be able to walk when I pray for my own healing, and for yours. New life, transformation of character, personality, behaviour, situation. Let's go for that instead, shall we? I think God's a lot more bothered about that. He's already raised the dead, so reinstating my dead brain cells probably isn't that big a deal anyway. What he really wants is for both you and I to understand more of who he is, who we are, and the wonder of what life together, and with him looks like. You can't do that while you're walking away from me in the opposite direction. Walking's for losers anyway.[11]

There is an element in this story that is often missing in discussions among theologians about disability, and that is moral indignation. Yes, God is a God who shows himself in vulnerability. But God is a God of justice who is implacably hostile to evil, who calls us to emulate his passion for justice. From the patronizing attitude Haydon had to put up with, through to the despicable treatment of disabled people in certain places throughout the world, Christians are called to be motivated not just by compassion but by passion. Sometimes effective change can take place only because of indignation against injustice. Wherever possible, disabled people need to be empowered to self-advocate, but we are all called to protest against injustice. Without that indignation we might be seen as passively capitulating, accepting the status quo when we should be the ones trying to undermine that status quo in order to bring about liberation.

As we know, we all need each other if we are to flourish, as opposed to just surviving. We want to be accepted as a part of a healing community that will stand in solidarity with us and cares about what happens to us. The Church claims to be such a community. We want to 'belong'. The Church also claims to be the only enabling community within which people can discover what it means to be truly human. It is to that community that we now turn.

9

The enabling community

The Church is the new community that takes its calling from the life of Christ. Formed in a spectacular way on the Day of Pentecost, the Church was (and is) a celebration of diversity. As people spoke out about the message of Jesus in languages they had never learned, others looked on in amazement, thinking they were drunk.

It was the day on which a bunch of confused and frightened disciples became the enabling community. Every disciple became a witness to the power of the risen Christ. It didn't matter who they were or what their background was, or whether they had an impairment. No conditions were placed on those who were part of the birth of the Church. People did not need to be 'cured'; in being filled with the Holy Spirit they entered into the healing that is one aspect of that greater salvation (*soteria*). Each person, as they were, became a powerful witness to the story of Jesus. Some, like Saul who later became Paul, had an impairment, but would be powerful witnesses to the resurrection of Christ. These people were not 'weak'. They were transformed people who had been empowered to become God's new society.

As Luke points out in his parable of the banquet, the ones who come to the party (representing the kingdom of God) are those with impairments (Luke 14.15–24). They come as they are; they do not have to be healed in order to be the honoured guests. This is a picture of disabled people not as weak and helpless but as preferable to those who claim to be too important to turn up. The world of ambition and self-importance is subverted by the world of apparent weakness. This passage is a shot across the bows for those who believe that the ultimate expression of the kingdom of God in the New World will be composed of 'normal' or even 'successful' people; God's preference may be so much more radical than that.

This has enormous implications when we consider the difference between a Christian perspective on disability and the other models[1] that are conventionally used to understand it. The social model, which focuses on exclusion and the need for political change, while being useful is undermined by the inclusion of disabled people in the New Community. This New Community upsets the status quo, challenging the traditional assumptions of the day and enabling disabled people to participate in God's New Society. On this day people found that whatever their bodies were like, they experienced a new way of being a person; they were to be included as they were in a society characterized by liberation, participation and salvation. Of course, their impairments might be cured by healing prayer if that was God's intention for them. But this was not necessary in order for them to experience the power and presence of God in their lives. The medical model, with its emphasis on curing the body, was undermined as Pentecost inaugurated a new way of being a person.

So the uniqueness of the Church's position is found in the Incarnation of Jesus, the resurrection of Christ and the birth of the New Community at the day of Pentecost. But there is another picture that reinforces the fact that Christian perspectives on disability are essentially about the gospel rather than about any model defined on secular lines. This is derived from one of the most potent images contained in the book of Revelation.

The scroll of history

Jean Vanier, in the conversation at the end of this book, says that for him the most basic problem exposed by the life of disabled people is the use and abuse of power. Christians are always cautious whenever people claim that the answer to their problems is more power. Christianity has at its heart the belief that true power is not ephemeral. It must stand up to the scrutiny of eternity. The events that take place in the throne room described in Revelation 5 make this plain.

Consider the scenario. The apostle John is being shown behind the scenes of human history. We have all lived our lives seeing them 'through a glass, darkly', with many unanswered questions, not only about world events but also about the way our own lives have taken shape. 'Why did my business fail?' 'Why did my child die?' 'What use was the period of depression I went through?' John is privileged to be at the unveiling of God's perspective on these things and also God's plans for the future of the world. For the first time John is about to see human history as salvation history – history from God's perspective.

God's perspective, and the answers that will satisfy human longing, are described as being contained in a scroll with seven seals. Who is worthy to open the scroll? Certainly no compromised and partial human being can undertake such a holy task. No one is found, and John weeps with frustration and disappointment. Then a voice is heard, which says that 'the Lion of the tribe of Judah' is the one that is worthy to open the scroll and reveal the meaning of history. But instead of a powerful lion, representing Jesus as the conqueror of sin and death, John sees a lamb which appears to have been killed. The lion symbolizes power, but it is the lamb – the crucified Christ – that takes the scroll and opens it. The figure of the lamb, with its connotations of sacrifice, passivity and death, is as far removed from the idea of power as one can get. But at that point a series of songs and acclamations break out in praise of the lamb:

'Worthy is the Lamb, who was slain, to receive power and wealth and wisdom and strength and honour and glory and praise!' Then I heard every creature in heaven and on earth and under the earth and on the sea, and all that is in them, saying: 'To him who sits on the throne and to the Lamb be praise and honour and glory and power, for ever and ever!'   (Rev. 5.12–13)

It turns out that the conquering lion and the sacrificial lamb refers to the same person, the risen and wounded Christ. But it is the latter figure to whom is attributed power, wealth, wisdom, strength, honour, glory and praise. It would not be surprising if these were associated with the lion, already a figure of power. But not only is the unveiling of history done by one who seems to characterize weakness, this person receives rewards that in our society are sought by, and promised to, those who are ambitious for power.

This passage shows that these rewards cannot be grasped. They are a gift. The only way to receive these gifts is to live the life of a servant, not as a person of power. The problem, as we have seen, is that a competitive society stereotypes this way of life as weak, viewing it with either ridicule or indifference. However, in this passage we also find that fake versions of these accolades exist that are ephemeral and illusory. Only those who live their lives on the pattern of the lamb will be given the true gifts that stand the test of eternity.

The radical difference between the secular view of power and the Christian perspective is that in the former, the world offers an option – *either* power *or* weakness. However, the Christian option is a long way from this. Since power and weakness are two sides of the same coin (the lion and the lamb are the same person), we are offered a vision of power *through* weakness. In other words, false power is subverted through weakness. *It is when the Church gets taken up with power and success that it becomes weak; when it serves the weak and welcomes them into its arms it becomes powerful and is most faithful to its message.* In Christianity those who are seen by the world as weak are only 'apparently weak'. As St Paul says, 'when I am weak, then I am strong' (2 Cor. 12.10).

To live as Jesus lived is, from this perspective, the way of true power. This is not the way of self-sufficiency or autonomy, but the laying down of one's life. But, as Jesus taught, those who have no power to start with find it much easier to live in this way than those with great prospects in the world who have to give them up, as in the story of the rich young ruler. To live in the way of Jesus is attractive for those who have nothing, or who have decided that they want nothing. But those who cling to their wealth and status face a daunting task.

In the Incarnation, God humbled himself and became a servant in order to show us what he was truly like. In the resurrection we see that the risen Christ identifies with disabled people and all who suffer, not requiring them to be 'cured' to be whole. Pentecost illustrates that disabled people are powerhouses of Christian witness. Then the picture of the lamb and the scroll shows us that false power is subverted through weakness.

Yes, Christians should fight passionately for and with disabled people so that they have access to justice and equality. But the world is deluded about its lust for power, and the Church cannot include this in its portrayal of the 'good life' for it has a far more radical message to portray.

The enabled life

Dietrich Bonhoeffer, the German theologian who opposed Hitler and later died as a martyr, spent some time in 1933 in a village called Bethel whose sole purpose was caring for disabled people and those who were ill. In a letter to his grandmother Julie, he talks of a church 'that still knows what the church can be about and what it cannot be about'. He continues:

> I have just come back from the worship service. It is an extraordinary sight, the whole church filled with crowds of epileptics and other ill persons, interspersed with the deaconesses and deacons who are there to help in case one of them falls; then there are elderly tramps who come in off the country roads, the theological students, the children from the lab school, doctors and pastors with their families. But the sick people dominate the picture, and they are keen listeners and participants.[2]

It was this experience that caused Bonhoeffer to reflect on how disability can teach us a great deal about what it means to be human. He focuses on those living with epilepsy:

> Their experience of life must be most extraordinary, not having control over their bodies, having to be resigned to the possibility of an attack at any moment. Today in church was the first time this really struck me, as I became aware of these moments. Their situation of being truly defenceless perhaps gives these people a much clearer insight into certain realities of human existence, the fact that we are basically defenceless, than can be possible for healthy persons. And it is just this abrupt alternation between standing there healthy and falling down sick which must be more conducive to this insight than being healthy all the time.[3]

Bonhoeffer was quite firm on the fact that this realization was nothing to do with sentiment. This church portrayed life as it was, rather than being an idealization of what it should be. In his essay on Bonhoeffer and disability, Bernd Wannenwetsch comments:

> Instead of understanding Bethel as a ghetto of love, but a ghetto nevertheless, Bonhoeffer grasped its significance as a place of revelation, a place which revealed the reality of universal Christian brotherhood. It was an embodied recognition that all human life is essentially feeble, defenceless and dependent, and so revealed neighbourly love as the matrix of all human sociality.[4]

But Bonhoeffer saw benevolence as a serious temptation for Christians; this must have been confusing for those who thought that in behaving in this way towards disabled people they were fulfilling the gospel. Bonhoeffer was all too aware that benevolence could turn out to be 'condescension instead of humility'. Wannenwetsch points out that the difference between neighbourly love and benevolence is important for the debate on inclusion, which we looked at earlier. What if, instead of powerful people conceding that 'weak disabled people' are persons in its fullest sense, perhaps we should ask the powerful to recognize that they will only discover *their* true humanity when they see themselves as vulnerable and in need of loving relationships? It is a very different message. The boot is on the other foot.

It is difficult for those with power to accept that they are vulnerable; it is just as difficult for those who have been promised power to accept that resurrection power, at least, comes with visible wounds. Certainly Bonhoeffer would agree with Hans Reinders that it is love and friendship that cause our humanity to blossom, and fear that prevents us from living the enabled life. We live in a disabling world. So it is ironic and disappointing that false religion, with its obsession with power, is one of the most disabling forces in the world.

The consequences for the Church

What, then, is the Church to be like? It must, first, examine itself as to whether it wants anything to do with disabled people. I remember a friend telling me that he had toured the country speaking to churches about their responsibilities under what was then the new Disability Discrimination Act. These included, in many cases, improving access to church buildings. He said to me, 'You would not believe how many church leaders sidled up to me afterwards and said, "What's the minimum we have to do to get away with this?"' They were not interested in disabled people. They preferred the status quo.

On another occasion I was at a conference where someone gave a lecture about disability and the Church. He projected a satellite picture showing his church and the surrounding neighbourhood. From local authority records he had found out who, in the immediate vicinity of the church, was a disabled person. On the image, each house that was the home of a disabled person had a red sticker on it. If that person went to the church he put a red sticker on the church. But while there were plenty of red stickers in the community, there were no red stickers on the picture of the church. The neighbourhood contained a number of people who had an impairment of one sort or another, but none of them went to church. The apostle Paul might question what kind of church this really was. Religious people went there, hymns were sung, prayers were said, sermons were preached, but a whole swathe of people was missing.

Paul was very keen on the metaphor of the Church as a human body, composed of different elements (1 Cor. 12.12–31). For the body to 'work', all the elements need to relate to one another properly. You can't have a body composed entirely of eyes or noses, and a body won't work without a heart. Paul knew that even the most modest parts of the body were necessary for it to function, despite some parts of the body being seen as important and others less so. In this image Paul saw the body as the Church community, but his view was that it was those who were considered by outsiders as less important or inferior that should be given 'the greater honour'. In other words, those who are disregarded and marginalized by the world are the most important in the Church. If they are missing, there is something wrong.

> The eye cannot say to the hand, 'I don't need you!' And the head cannot say to the feet, 'I don't need you!' On the contrary, those parts of the body that seem to be weaker are indispensable, and the parts that we think are less honourable we treat with special honour. And the parts that are unpresentable are treated with special modesty, while our presentable parts need no special treatment. But God has put the body together, giving greater honour to the parts that lacked it, so that there should be no division in the body, but that its parts should have equal concern for each other. If one part suffers, every part suffers with it; if one part is honoured, every part rejoices with it.
>
> (1 Cor. 12.21–26)

It is all too easy for the local church to become a club. We invite friends for dinner and they invite us back. But, Jesus says, reciprocity is not the basis of the kingdom of God. We are to love those who do not love us back. In that way we create community rather than merely maintaining it.

One problem is the professionalization that is applied at church. We have made 'giving God our very best' an exclusion zone. Those who sing do so perfectly in tune, those who read are embarrassed if they make a mistake, those who preach are meant to be profound and witty at the same time. There are, of course, churches where the preachers, choir and readers are appalling and grimly persist to the boredom of the three people and a dog in the congregation. But that is not the point. We often see involvement in the church as restricted to the competent. Churches are frequently run by a small group of committed people while others sit on the sidelines and cannot find their place despite the fact that they have gifts to offer.

But the more that friendship is at the heart of church life, the more room there is for difference. A student of mine is doing a research project on disability issues, and she told me recently of a church in her area where there was a young boy who raced round during services and caused a bit of noise. He was living with autism. 'Doesn't anybody mind?' I asked. 'No,' she said. 'About a quarter of the church are related to him anyway, so nobody minds.' The more the church is about relationship rather than about performance, the easier it is for us to be accepted and blessed.

There is another way of looking at this. It is beautifully described by the apostle Paul: 'from now on we regard no one from a worldly point of view. Even though we once regarded Christ in this way, we do so no longer' (2 Cor. 5.16). In other words, Christians have a different perspective on other people.

The great Christian leader John Stott travelled the world tirelessly, meeting people and preaching. He had a remarkable facility for remembering people and as a result many viewed him as a friend. He had a lifelong ministry at All Souls, Langham

Place in London, and people would come from all over the world to hear him speak. After one service he was shaking hands with the congregation as they left – hundreds of people were at the service and wanted to greet him. His young assistant was standing behind him all the time. After everyone had gone, he asked how John could be so patient with people and greet each one as a friend. His response was: 'As I shake their hand I remember that each one is made in the image of God and is a person for whom Christ died.'

That is what Paul means. When we meet a person it is not whether they can see or hear, whether they have epileptic seizures or profound intellectual impairments, that matters. It is that they are a person of infinite worth and should be treated with respect and love.

What God wants is a 'Church for all'. Not a Church *for* disabled people, nor a Church that *includes* disabled people, but a Church for all. It is for anybody who is willing to love and be loved, discovering in the process that they are, and have always been, God's gift to the world.

10

A conversation between
Roy McCloughry and Jean Vanier[1]

About Jean Vanier[2]

Jean Vanier was born on 10 September 1928 in Geneva, Switzerland, where his father, General Georges Vanier, was on a diplomatic mission. Most of his early schooling was in England, where he lived until the outbreak of the Second World War when his parents sent him, with his four brothers and one sister, back to Canada.

Two years later, the young Jean decided to enter the Royal Naval College in England, although at the time he was too young to become a soldier. He assisted his mother in her Red Cross work in Paris after the liberation, helping with those returning from the concentration camps. In 1945, Jean received his officer's commission and began his naval career.

Despite the promising career path that lay in front of him, he was more and more drawn into prayer and reflection on what might be God's call for him. In 1950 he resigned from the Navy in order to study philosophy and theology at the Institut Catholique in Paris. There he met Father Thomas Philippe, a Dominican priest and professor who was to become Jean's spiritual mentor and friend.

In 1963, having published his doctoral thesis on Aristotle, he returned to Canada to teach at the University of Toronto. Again, he decided against the security of a career and left both job and homeland to join Father Thomas Philippe, who had become chaplain to a small institution for men with developmental disabilities, in France: the Val Fleury in Trosly-Breuil. In 1964 Jean decided to settle in Trosly to live with people with an intellectual disability. He bought a small house and named it 'L'Arche', the French word for Noah's Ark.

Though heavily involved in the rapidly growing community, Jean began to address conferences and host retreats around the world. In 1969, following a retreat in Ontario, the first community of L'Arche in North America was founded. The next year, again after a visit by Jean, a L'Arche community in India was founded. In 1968 Jean Vanier co-founded Faith and Sharing. In these communities, families who have a member with a disability and their friends meet once a month for prayer and mutual support and celebration. Three years later, a pilgrimage to Lourdes of 12,000 people with developmental disabilities, and their friends and families, led to the co-founding of Faith and Light with Marie-Hélène Mathieu. This sister pilgrimage movement brings people with an intellectual disability, and their family members and friends, together for regular gatherings and periodic pilgrimages of friendship, prayer and celebration. In the early 1990s, Jean Vanier founded Intercordia, which provides university students with an accredited cross-cultural experience in social education and personal growth among poor or marginalized peoples in the developing world.

L'Arche was spreading rapidly. Jean, becoming aware that it was important to call forth others who could lead, handed over the leadership of the International Federation of L'Arche Communities to the first International Coordinator in 1981. He continued to sit as Founder on the International Council of L'Arche, and also continued to travel a great deal, encouraging L'Arche communities and giving spiritual accompaniment and guidance to the many people who come to him from within and beyond L'Arche.

Jean Vanier has received numerous awards, among which are the French Legion of Honour, Companion of the Order of Canada, the Rabbi Gunther Plaut Humanitarian Award 2001 and the Chicago Catholic Theological Union 'Blessed are the Peace-makers' award 2006.

Today, Jean Vanier still travels the world to give retreats and conferences; the 1998 CBC Massey Lectures are just one prominent example. In 2006 he travelled to Africa, Indonesia and the USA. His books have been translated into 29 languages. Jean continues to live in the first L'Arche community in Trosly-Breuil, France.

The conversation

Roy: Jean, what is the starting point for thinking about disability?

Jean: Maybe I will begin by saying first of all – the danger in the Church is an idealized view of the human being whereas we are all prone to sickness and to death, therefore to disability or weakness, and this is becoming more prevalent today as we discover people ageing and so on. So I would tend to say that disability pushes us to see what it is to be human. Disabled people[3] are calling us to be attentive to love which is an attentiveness to listening, an attentiveness to presence which is essential when you are living with people who cannot talk. It means a sort of proximity and you learn to be present to people and to be in communion with them. So I find that disabled people lead us on a path, which is the Christian path, which teaches us to love with tenderness, listening and openness. This is very different from our individualistic society today. So being with them, they are teaching us something which we should all know but which we don't. Disabled people are not in a separate category from the rest of us. Obviously we are all human, however deep the disability is, but in some mysterious way being with them, they are leading us on the path of what it means to be Christian, what it means to be spiritual.

Roy: One of the important things then is that we find ways of talking about disability which include us all rather than seeing them as 'others'. But when you talk about being present with disabled people this assumes that you learn about Christian love by living with them. Yet that is rare in the contemporary Church in the West. Does that mean the Church is in fundamental difficulties and is missing out on something essential because of this?

Jean: I would say that the Church, if it is not attentive to disabled people who are teaching us to be attentive to others, might then begin to focus too much on the institutional. Yet the main vision of Jesus is that we should love one another and announce good news to the poor. I believe that disabled people are a door that opens us up to that Christian vision.

Roy: Do you think that disabled people have something different to say to us than somebody who is impoverished but abled?

Jean: People with profound disabilities have a way of opening up and entering into a relationship, which attracts us deeply. Of course, people have all kinds of impairments and so what I am saying here is not true of all, but with those who have a profound mental disability there is a sort of cry for affection and a simplicity which you also find sometimes with a child. The child breaks downs our barriers and calls us to an attentiveness, to communion. So in a way which is profoundly human they lead us into what it is to be most human. I think disabled people yearn for this communion whereas people who are so-called normal are frequently yearning for power and success. They touch something very deep with their simplicity, their trust and so on. It can be a healing of the heart.

Roy: Are we focused here on people with profound intellectual impairments rather than other kinds of impairments? Is that what makes you talk about the child within, because there are many people with impairments who may feel that concept belittles them?

Jean: I think particularly of those with intellectual disabilities. But in the same way someone who is deaf or blind, obliges us to be attentive to him or her. But they haven't the same cry which you find with the child who has not developed his or her powers of individualism, success or power.

Roy: Is power the touchstone really for you?

Jean: I would say that is the touchstone. There are laws of nature and God is humble in front of nature but when somebody is being excluded because of a fragility then there is an attentiveness of God towards the excluded. That does not mean to say that he is not attentive to those who want power, but people who want power do not always want love and communion.

Roy: Does that mean that Western Christianity in particular has not grappled with the root, with the heart of theology, in the way that it should?

Jean: If we are talking about theology, I would say yes, because Jesus teaches something about humility whereas if you look in other religions, God can appear always the powerful one. With Christology we have the Word becoming flesh and then a servant God. But when we work with Muslims or Hindus, as we do, they discover another vision of God through the practical reality of living with disabled people. At the heart of the mystery are the two realities: the servant Jesus but also the mystery that being wounded, we are healed by his wounds. The mystery of Christology is not just the servant Jesus, the one kneeling at our feet, but also the Jesus who accepted to go to the very end, and through his death brought life. This is important for a lot of people with severe impairments and for those who are suffering. Isaiah 53 is important here.

Roy: And do you put as much weight on the significance of the risen Christ's wounds as disability theologian Nancy Eiesland has done?

Jean: I would tend to say yes. I am always touched by the fact that the very first words of the risen Christ in John's Gospel are 'Where is your pain? Why are you suffering? Why are you crying?' It wasn't 'Wow, our risen leader!' As a leader, his first words were of compassion: 'Where is your pain?' So the risen leader is teaching us to be attentive to pain.

Roy: And that is different from the modern Church's view of healing, isn't it? Often the Church's view seems to see healing as turning a disabled person into one who is not. It seems to be the medical model all over again but in religious language and practice. What is your own view?

Jean: Yes, I fear something which is similar to when you mentioned the medical model. For me the important thing with people with severe disabilities is to be present for them, to be revealed to them and then to gradually help them to discover it is okay to be them and then discover what is most fundamental in them. As to healing I have had experiences which really hurt me. One was in Beirut. A priest who was known as a healer held a meeting. There were hundreds of mothers holding severely disabled children, really severely disabled. Yes, there were a few healings but nobody said to those women, 'Your children are beautiful', and so there is this model that you have to be healed.

Roy: So how should we approach this? Nowadays we get the impression that if God is revealed in power God is most present with us. Whereas what you are saying is that when we accept that God is revealed in weakness then God is most present in us. So how do we actually change that way of seeing God?

Jean: The only thing I can say for the moment is that people who have the experience of being prison chaplains, hospital chaplains or people living with children, find that when they have lived this experience with a quality of love which flows from vulnerability, then they can bring that into their theology. But my feeling is that many begin with a bad vision of theology, and frequently, at least in the Catholic Church, with a vision which is almost a philosophical view of God, an Aristotelian view of God, a view which begins with the power of God. The revelation of God as the one who emptied himself of glory to become a slave is, in some way, put aside or made something exceptional rather than as the heart of the matter.

Roy: So where does that distorted view of theology come from? What is generating it?

Jean: It goes back to our view of what it means to be human. What I mean is that we begin in life as children who are very vulnerable. There is that beautiful relationship between father and mother and child which is only dependence. But then the child must grow and she must, like everyone else, enter into society. There is something very deep in the human psyche of the need to prove that we are better than others. My identity can become that of 'the one who wins'. Now unless Christianity counteracts that through the vision of who Jesus is, how does that person grow? Where are the people in our celebrity society who will model what it means to go in the right direction?

Roy: Is one of our problems that we find modern life does not encourage prayer?

Jean: Yes. My own feeling is that the Church can quickly fall into a fascination with numbers and things like that and therefore entertain an element of power. But if you read through Acts, the first disciples were humble because they were being moved by the Spirit and did not quite know where they were going. Today the Church is different. It is holding on to something which is very fundamental for the human being, which is the need for success.

Roy: Why do people always want disabled people to change? Some people even assume that in the New World one of the fundamental changes will be that disabled people will be changed but the rest of us will not, as if they need to be 'brought up to scratch'.

Jean: I think people don't quite know what it means to love. How does a child love; how do they see people? We assume that to love is to do things for people. So it follows that the more capable you are, the more you can do and therefore you are better than others. But what if to love is to know how to enter into communion, to be in relationship – which implies humility – and how to see the gift of the other, how to see the gift of a person with a disability? How to discover what is apparently at the bottom of humanity can teach us a lot of things. It is always true that the ways of the world are different from the ways of God. It is very striking that Jesus says, 'If somebody loves me and follows my commandments, I will pray the Father and he will give them another Paraclete, the Spirit of Truth, which the world cannot receive.' They cannot receive because the world is a place of competition and rivalry. If they have to prove that they are better then they cannot receive. I can only receive if I have touched my brokenness, incapacity or difficulty in loving others. I need Jesus. I need his help.

Roy: Is that brokenness just to do with our human weakness and our vulnerability? Or is it also to do morally with our sin? Those are different, aren't they?

Jean: Fundamentally, sin is the refusal of God as Saviour. So they are interrelated. The way they are perceived is slightly different or the way we talk about them is different, but basically they are the same thing. It is the rejection of the fact that I need help from God because I am a broken person. I need help. I have difficulty with loving people. I need to change. I need to be transformed. Sin and these things are very close together.

I would say they are the same thing but seen from different sides. For me, original sin, if I may use that term, is that the first movement of the human being after that relationship with the mother, can be the need to have power. But Adam and Eve, before sin came, accepted the status of being a child of God. These two elements of sin and wanting power are intimately linked.

Roy: The Bible doesn't seem to be very clear when it comes to disability. Sometimes it uses the language of disability to describe judgement. At other times it seems to suggest that there is a link between disability and sin. What do you think?

Jean: Humanity is always moving, and what we are saying today is even different from what was said a hundred years ago.

Roy: So is it seeing the good in people that matters to you?

Jean: This is the beginning of the heart of the matter. Discovering the good in people. I see this with people who come here with no faith; I am talking about disabled people. It is the same thing with the sisters I work with because they have been humiliated by the way people have looked at them. Then gradually by living together and eating together, it is revealed to them that 'you are precious'. Instead of seeing them as damned, we see there is something beautiful in them. You can see that I am walking on a tightrope. (*Laughter*)

If you say something and then people reject it, then the Church will not see what it could see today. The Church could see today that disabled people have something to offer the Church. St Paul says that those who are the weakest are indispensable to the Church.

Frances Young, the Methodist pastor and theologian from Birmingham, talks about that and it is beautiful. When you are confronted by Arthur, her son, who is so handicapped, it is about recognizing that Jesus is there in his deep disability. We are not there to make people like Arthur normal.

Roy: Some are talking about an increased intolerance towards disabled people because genetics will be able to give us a lot more information about the health of the foetus than we currently have. So parents who choose to have a child who they know is going to be disabled may risk the state denying them any support. In other words, the ultimate end of a consumer society is that people become commodities themselves. Such a society may only tolerate 'normal' people who do not use up scarce resources.

Jean: The Church began with martyrs and maybe these will be martyrs. You have put your finger on something which is the greatest danger today. A mother who wants to maintain and keep her child, against society saying I will not give you social security. So will the Christian community be there to support that mother? That is the way society is moving and it is moving in a normative and competitive way, so the weakest, who should be protected, are not being protected.

Roy: Is the Church too weak in its own understanding of what humanity is, to be able to resist this?

Jean: Yes. It is difficult that we use the word Church because you find wonderful people in the Church, yet you find others, sometimes the more significant people, like the bishops. In the Catholic Church lay people are being pushed to study theology rather than being encouraged to do something like going to live with people who have Alzheimer's. Alzheimer's is seen to be a professional business but maybe it is people with Alzheimer's who will teach us about what it is to be human and what it is to be Christian. Learning about theology is good, of course, and we need to do it. But I said something which I shouldn't have said in a meeting yesterday. I said that I am sometimes frightened about people wanting Jesus but not wanting to grow in love. They didn't like that because they like the Jesus of Power.

Roy: A superman.

Jean: We can believe, but to go and live with people with Alzheimer's, that's nuts. Sometimes we learn most when we join Mary at the foot of the cross.

Roy: Does that mean that one of the problems we have, for instance, is that we always want to have things explained rather than leaving them at the foot of the cross?

Jean: In point of fact, when you live with disabled people, you experience something which other people cannot understand rationally – they have not lived the experience. We are coming back to those words, 'The spirit of truth which the world cannot understand.' When Jesus stands up and cries out, 'Let he who is thirsty come to me and drink', so thirst comes as we go down, but it is also the thirst for God.

Roy: So basically anyone listening to you would say that being involved with disabled people is the heart of the gospel. It is not some separate theology. It is the heart of the gospel.

Jean: It is the heart of the gospel, which is about an acknowledgement of weakness. We cannot do it ourselves. We need help. We need God. We need a Saviour.

Roy: If it is the heart of the gospel, then it should have a missional component to it, not just be for the Church. But if, as you have said, disabled people are the prophets to a competitive and ambitious world, how does the world hear them?

Jean: Today we find quite a lot of couples between the ages of 35 and 45 who are disappointed in the need for power and who are beginning to ask what it means to be human. I see army officers who are leaving the army and are now wanting training in heading up homes for elderly people. There is a movement which is growing because this need for power has gone too far. Some are beginning to sense that there must be another road and for some that will be a Christian road. But essentially it is a realization that to be human we have to accept our vulnerability and the vulnerabilities of others. Many are asking fundamental questions about the major difference in our world between rich and poor, with two billion people living in slum areas.

Roy: You have been talking about presence and experience and being in relationship and yet you read academic books, you address academic conferences, you have got a mind which is big and you love reading and thinking. Do you sometimes think all this is very well, here is another paper on disability, but what they need is experience, what I have experienced. How would you convey to those people who are making a career, a powerful career out of disability and theology, that really this is not the way to go?

Jean: It is really useful for the Church. We need good theologians, we need good books and it will fall into the hands of this person and that person. It's like the whole reality of prophecy. Turn your eyes away from normality and the winning in the Church, converting everybody else to something else. Not seeing people who are old as useless but maybe they can teach us something. We need the theologians, we need them. It is vital because otherwise we just remain on the spiritual element. I am part of a group, Intercordia. We send young people to Africa and we oblige all of them after a year to write a document on how they have been changed, to move from an emotional reality which they have lived in a village in Africa, to move from the spiritual emotion to the intellectual and the understanding. There the theologians are absolutely necessary, such as Thomas Reynolds and yourself.

Every year, we have about 30 future priests who come here and I meet them after they have stayed a month and pretty well all of them say, 'I feel transformed', so they then have to read about what transformation is. They have to live with the emotion but they also need to intellectualize it. The danger is to say that the Church has all the knowledge it needs already and is not looking for any more prophets. But the prophets – they are the disabled people.

Appendix 1
The charter for intercessors

The following series of 20 points is intended to guide those who are praying for healing. It was published in an earlier book, *Making a World of Difference*,[1] but as some have found it a helpful guide to best practice I have included it here too. It can be used as an aid when training those who will be praying for others.

1 The focus of the healing ministry is the encounter between God who heals and those people who bring their requests to God. Intercessors facilitate that encounter.

2 Every person who asks for prayer for healing should be treated with respect and dignity. They should not be embarrassed or exploited, nor should their wishes be ignored. This is particularly important when the ministry of healing takes place in a public place.

3 Those who offer prayer for healing should do so with integrity. Those who come for prayer should do so without seeking to manipulate or in any way undermine those who pray for them. Mutual respect is essential to both intercessor and supplicant.

4 If an intercessor uses a particular symbol in prayer (such as laying on of hands or anointing with oil), the significance of this should be explained to the supplicant and their consent obtained. The supplicant should, at any point, have the freedom to stop whatever is going on.

5 No pressure should be put on a supplicant, by any means, to state that they have been healed. They should feel that they have the freedom to say that they do not think that they are, to the best of their knowledge.

6 God heals as an expression of his radical freedom to do as he wishes. Healing witnesses to the wholeness associated with the reign of God and points forward in hope to the new world coming. In healing we may have a bodily experience of renewal, but we may also have an experience of the love of God who is with us, or a change in our own attitudes to the situation in which we find ourselves. Healing is not the same as cure.

7 Healing is not a matter of success or failure. Praying for somebody shows that they are cared for, included in the family of God, and shows solidarity with them. Neither those who pray nor those prayed for should carry this additional burden.

8 Where testimony is given the supplicant should be able to deliver their testimony in their own words and from their own perspective. No pressure should be brought to bear on them, and neither should testimony be given on their behalf, either in spoken or written form, without their consent.

9 Prayer for healing does not complete the Church's responsibility. It may be important to refer people to continuing pastoral care. Offering prayer for healing means that we are willing to follow people up, ensuring that the Church expresses continuity of appropriate care.

10 It is also important to recognize that there is a link between healing prayer and social justice, since those in need may also be the victims of injustice or discrimination. The love of justice is also a sign of our love for God.

11 Intercessors should see themselves as part of a team. It is helpful if prayer is offered by people in pairs. This enables responsibility to be shared, perspectives to be discussed and each person to receive support from the other.

12 Prayer takes place in a wider context than the Church. Lay people or church leaders who are intercessors in a healing context should see themselves as a part of a team, which includes physicians, psychiatrists, social workers, counsellors

and other healthcare professionals who are also exercising gifts given to them by God. Similarly, those who work in a medical environment or in social services should not ignore the ministry of the local church.

13 Many claims to healing are ambiguous and cannot be verified. Where there is a claim that someone has been healed in a way that is verifiable, this should be investigated and confirmed by medical authorities. Jesus told the leper to 'show himself to the priest' in order that the healing be confirmed. When making claims to healing we should be willing to have them confirmed by those who are medically trained, whether or not they share a Christian world-view.

14 Where someone comes forward for healing prayer with an overt impairment it should not be assumed that they have come for prayer for that impairment. The supplicant may not perceive their impairment to be a problem that needs healing. There is no substitute for careful listening.

15 People with disabilities may also be intercessors for healing. The Church betrays its calling if it conducts its public healing ministry in a way that is not accessible to people with disabilities. The integrity of the healing ministry cannot be separated from access to that ministry.

16 It may be extremely harmful to be told that one is not healed because of sin (either one's own or that of previous generations), or because of lack of faith. In the majority of instances the person praying for healing cannot possibly know that this is true. It may be true that a person is struggling morally or with their faith. Such a person needs support, encouragement and care rather than accusation. If there are problems, these should be dealt with privately in the context of pastoral care.

17 Intercessors who offer prayer for healing today may be those who want prayer for healing, today or tomorrow. Similarly, those who ask for prayer today may also be those who pray for others tomorrow.

18 Intercessors who pray for healing and do so as a permanent ministry in their local church need pastoral care and accountability to exercise their ministry with confidence and integrity. They may also face situations that drain them physically, emotionally and spiritually. They need not only to receive pastoral care themselves, but to retreat to places where they can find refreshment and new energy for their ministry.

19 Wherever possible, those people who have a ministry that is recognized by the local church should be commissioned and welcomed into that ministry by the local church.

20 Where there are valid criticisms of the conduct of a church's healing ministry these must be taken seriously and not dismissed. The Church will always make mistakes but can only grow in its ministry if they are heeded and lessons learned from them.

Appendix 2
The Lausanne statement on disability[1]

People with disabilities form one of the largest minority groups in the world, estimated to exceed 600 million. [The latest World Health Organization figures put this at over one billion.] The majority of these live in the least developed countries and are among the poorest of the poor. Although physical or mental impairment is a part of their daily experience, most are also disabled by social attitudes, injustice and lack of access to resources. Serving people with disabilities does not stop with medical care or social provision; it involves fighting alongside them, those who care for them and their families, for inclusion and equality, both in society and in the Church. God calls us to mutual friendship, respect, love and justice.

1 Let us rise up as Christians worldwide to reject cultural stereo-types, for as the apostle Paul commented, 'we no longer regard anyone from a human point of view'. Made in the image of God we all have gifts God can use in his service. We commit both to minister to people with disabilities and to receive the ministry they have to give.

2 We encourage church and mission leaders to think, not only of mission *among* those with a disability but to recognize, affirm and facilitate the missional calling of believers with disabilities themselves as part of the body of Christ.

3 We are grieved that so many people with disabilities are told that their impairment is due to personal sin, lack of faith or unwillingness to be healed. We deny that the Bible teaches this as a universal truth. Such false teaching is pastorally insensitive and spiritually disabling; it adds the burden of

guilt and frustrated hopes to the other barriers that people with disabilities face.

4 We commit ourselves to make our churches places of inclusion and equality for people with disabilities and to stand alongside them in resisting prejudice and in advocating for their needs in wider society.

Notes

1 Two worlds

1 Andy Calder, 'To belong I need to be missed', *Journal of Religion, Disability and Health*, 16(3), 2012.

2 A story and a meditation

1 Statistics from the World Health Organization (Fact Sheet 999). See <www.who.int/mediacentre/factsheets/fs999/en/index.html>.

2 Those wishing to know more about epilepsy can find out more from Epilepsy Action <www.epilepsy.org.uk>.

3 Some years ago I did this and sent off my licence to the DVLA. I received a handwritten note in reply, thanking me for being a 'good citizen' and having integrity. It made me wonder just how many people do hand their licence back!

4 This word is usually inappropriate as a description of what happens when someone experiences a seizure, but it seems appropriate here given the context.

5 Talking of someone as 'an epileptic' is seen as offensive as it defines them by his or her condition. They are 'a person with epilepsy' or 'a person living with epilepsy'.

6 According to the World Health Organization Fact Sheet *Epilepsy: Social Consequences and Economic Aspects* (2001). See <https://apps.who.int/inf-fs/en/fact166.html>.

7 In Mark Greene (ed.), *Pocket Prayers for Work* (London: Church House Publishing, 2004), pp. 40–1.

3 Disability in perspective

1 Hans S. Reinders, *Receiving the Gift of Friendship: Profound Disability, Theological Anthropology and Friendship* (Grand Rapids, MI: Eerdmans, 2008), p. 140.

2 Reinders, *Receiving the Gift of Friendship*, p. 142.

3 Reinders, *Receiving the Gift of Friendship*, p. 143.

125

4 Creation

1 See Hans S. Reinders, *Receiving the Gift of Friendship: Profound Disability, Theological Anthropology and Ethics* (Grand Rapids, MI: Eerdmans, 2008), p. 101.

2 Dietrich Bonhoeffer, *Ethics*, tr. Reinhard Krauss, Charles C. West and Douglas W. Scott (Minneapolis, MN: Augsburg Fortress Press, 2005), p. 193.

3 Hans Reinders, *The Future of the Disabled in Liberal Society: An Ethical Analysis* (Notre Dame, IN: University of Notre Dame Press, 2000).

4 John Swinton, 'Forgetting whose we are: theological reflections on personhood, faith and dementia', *Journal of Religion, Disability and Health*, 11(1), 2007, p. 54.

5 Tom Reynolds, *Vulnerable Communion: A Theology of Disability and Hospitality* (Grand Rapids, MI: Brazos Press, 2008).

5 Compromise

1 On this see the charter for intercessors in Appendix 1, and also the reference to this in the excerpt from the Lausanne Covenant in Appendix 2.

2 See <www.time-to-change.org.uk/mental-health-statistics-facts>.

6 Covenant

1 Christopher J. H. Wright, *Old Testament Ethics for the People of God* (Downers Grove, IL: IVP, 2004), p. 173.

2 Christopher J. H. Wright, *Deuteronomy*, New International Bible Commentary, Old Testament Series (Carlisle: Paternoster Press, 1996), pp. 271–2 (italics in the original), quoted in Wright, *Old Testament Ethics*, pp. 174–5.

3 On this see William J. Webb, *Slaves, Women and Homosexuals: Exploring the Hermeneutics of Cultural Analysis* (Leicester: IVP, 2001); also Roy McCloughry and Wayne Morris, *Making a World of Difference: Christian Reflections on Disability* (London: SPCK, 2002).

4 Colleen C. Grant, 'Reinterpreting the healing narratives', in Nancy L. Eiesland and Don E. Saliers (eds), *Human Disability and the Service of God: Reassessing Religious Practice* (Nashville, TN: Abingdon Press, 1998), p. 80.

5 Grant, 'Reinterpreting the healing narratives', p. 84.
6 Nancy Eiesland, *The Disabled God: Towards a Liberatory Theology of Disability* (Nashville, TN: Abingdon Press, 1994), p. 89.
7 Eiesland, *The Disabled God*, p. 100.

7 Completion

1 Stanley J. Grenz, *Theology for the Community of God* (Nashville, TN: Broadman and Holman, 1994), p. 144.
2 C. S. Lewis, *The Last Battle* (London: HarperCollins Children's Books, 2007).

8 Healing and cure

1 Karl Barth, *Church Dogmatics*, II/1 (Edinburgh: T & T Clark, 1957), p. 257.
2 See Thomas Smail's article on the Fulcrum website, 'Towards a Theology of Healing' <www.fulcrum-anglican.org.uk/news/2007/20070417smail.cfm?doc=204>.
3 On this see Justine Allain-Chapman, *Resilient Pastors: The Role of Adversity in Healing and Growth* (London: SPCK, 2012).
4 Henri Nouwen, *The Wounded Healer: Ministry in Contemporary Society* (London: Darton, Longman and Todd, 2004).
5 Allain-Chapman, *Resilient Pastors*, p. 107.
6 John Hull, *In the Beginning There was Darkness* (London: SCM Press, 2001).
7 Nancy Eiesland, 'Sacramental bodies', *Journal of Religion, Disability and Health*, 13(3/4), 2009, pp. 236–46.
8 Eiesland, 'Sacramental bodies'.
9 Personal communication to the author, 4 December 2012.
10 Nancy Mairs, *Plaintext* (Tucson: University of Arizona Press, 1986), p. 20.
11 At the time of writing Haydon's blog is not accessible publicly, just distributed to a few friends and colleagues.

9 The enabling community

1 On this, see Amos Yong, *The Bible, Disability and the Church: A New Vision for the People of God* (Grand Rapids, MI: Eerdmans, 2011).

2 Dietrich Bonhoeffer, 'Letter to Julie Bonhoeffer', 20 August 1933, in Brian Brock and John Swinton (eds), *Disability in the Christian Tradition: A Reader* (Grand Rapids, MI: Eerdmans, 2012), p. 370.

3 Bonhoeffer, 'Letter to Julie Bonhoeffer', p. 370.

4 Bernd Wannenwetsch, '"My strength is made perfect in weakness": Bonhoeffer and the war over disabled life', in Brock and Swinton (eds), *Disability in the Christian Tradition*, pp. 353–90.

10 A conversation between Roy McCloughry and Jean Vanier

1 This conversation took place on 13 June 2012 at Jean Vanier's home in Trosly-Breuil, France.

2 This biography is taken from the L'Arche website <www.larche. org/jean-vanier-founder-of-l-arche.en-gb.23.13.content.htm>.

3 It is important to recognize throughout that Jean Vanier has worked and lived alongside people with profound intellectual disabilities for many years. When he refers to 'disabled people' or uses similar phrases, he is often referring to people with intellectual disabilities and not always to people with other kinds of impairment.

Appendix 1: The charter for intercessors

1 Roy McCloughry and Wayne Morris, *Making a World of Difference: Christian Perspectives on Disability* (London: SPCK, 2002), pp. 112–14. This is the original version and I have not altered it to reflect further discussion on healing in Chapter 8 of this book.

Appendix 2: The Lausanne statement on disability

1 The Lausanne Movement is a global expression of contemporary evangelicalism. The Lausanne Congress took place in Cape Town in 2010 and this is the statement on disability contained in the resulting Cape Town Commitment – part 2, section IIB, para. 4.

Further reading

There are many wonderful books addressing the issues raised by disability from a Christian perspective, and I have drawn attention to some of them here. Those with an asterisk (*) by them are less challenging and more accessible than those without. All of them are worth studying closely!

Allain-Chapman, Justine, *Resilient Pastors: The Role of Adversity in Healing and Growth* (London: SPCK, 2012).

Avalos, Hector, Melcher, Sarah J. and Shipper, Jeremy (eds), *This Abled Body: Rethinking Disabilities in Biblical Studies* (Atlanta, GA: Society of Biblical Literature, 2007).

Block, Jennie Weiss, *Copious Hosting: A Theology of Access for People with Disabilities* (London: Continuum, 2002).

Brock, Brian and Swinton, John (eds), *Disability in the Christian Tradition: A Reader* (Grand Rapids, MI: Eerdmans, 2012).

* Bryden, Christine, *Dancing with Dementia: My Story of Living Positively with Dementia* (London: Jessica Kingsley, 2005).

* Bryden, Christine, *Who Will I Be When I Die?* (London: Jessica Kingsley, 2012).

Creamer, Deborah Beth, *Disability and Christian Theology: Embodied Limits and Constructive Possibilities* (Oxford: Oxford University Press, 2009).

Edmonds, Matt, *A Theological Diagnosis: A New Direction on Genetic Therapy, 'Disability' and the Ethics of Healing* (London: Jessica Kingsley, 2011).

Eiesland, Nancy L., *The Disabled God: Towards a Liberatory Theology of Disability* (Nashville, TN: Abingdon Press, 1994).

Eiesland, Nancy L. and Saliers, Don E. (eds), *Human Disability and the Service of God: Reassessing Religious Practice* (Nashville, TN: Abingdon Press, 1998).

Gillebrand, John, *Disabled Church – Disabled Society: The Implications of Autism for Philosophy, Theology and Politics* (London: Jessica Kingsley, 2010).

* Hauerwas, Stanley and Vanier, Jean, *Living Gently in a Violent World* (Downers Grove, IL: IVP, 2008).
* Hull, John M., *In the Beginning There was Darkness* (London: SCM Press, 2001).
* McCloughry, Roy and Morris, Wayne, *Making a World of Difference: Christian Reflections on Disability* (London: SPCK, 2004).
Morris, Wayne, *Theology Without Words: Theology in the Deaf Community* (Aldershot: Ashgate, 2008).
* Nouwen, Henri, *The Wounded Healer: Ministry in Contemporary Society* (London: Darton, Longman and Todd, 1994).
* Nouwen, Henri, *The Road to Daybreak: A Spiritual Journey* (London: Darton, Longman and Todd, 1997).
* Nouwen, Henri, *Adam: God's Beloved* (Cincinnati, OH: Franciscan Media, 2007).
Reinders, Hans, *The Future of the Disabled in a Liberal Society: An Ethical Analysis* (Notre Dame, IN: Notre Dame Press, 2000).
Reinders, Hans, *Receiving the Gift of Friendship: Profound Disability, Theological Anthropology and Ethics* (Grand Rapids, MI: Eerdmans, 2008).
* Reinders, Hans (ed.), *The Paradox of Disability* (Grand Rapids, MI: Eerdmans, 2010).
Reynolds, Thomas E., *Vulnerable Communion: A Theology of Disability and Communion* (Grand Rapids, MI: Brazos Press, 2008).
Swinton, John, *Dementia: Living in the Memories of God* (Grand Rapids, MI: Eerdmans, 2012).
Swinton, John (ed.), *Critical Reflections on Stanley Hauerwas' Theology of Disability: Disabling Society, Enabling Theology* (Binghamton, NY: Haworth Pastoral Press, 2004).
* Temple, Gordon and Ball, Lin, *Enabling Church: A Bible-based Resource Towards the Full Inclusion of Disabled People* (London: SPCK, 2012).
* Vanier, Jean, *The Broken Body: Journey into Wholeness* (London: Darton, Longman and Todd, 1988).
* Vanier, Jean, *From Brokenness to Community: The Wit Lectures* (Mahwah, NJ: Paulist Press, 1992).
* Vanier, Jean, *Becoming Human* (London: Darton, Longman and Todd, 1999).

* Vanier, Jean, *Befriending the Stranger* (London: Darton, Longman and Todd, 2005).

Yong, Amos, *Theology and Down Syndrome: Reimagining Disability in Late Modernity* (Waco, TX: Baylor University Press, 2007).

Yong, Amos, *The Bible, Disability and the Church: A New Vision for the People of God* (Grand Rapids, MI: Eerdmans, 2011).

* Young, Frances, *Encounter with Mystery: Reflections on L'Arche and Living with Disability* (London: Darton, Longman and Todd, 1997).

* Young, Frances, *Brokenness and Blessing: Towards a Biblical Spirituality* (London: Darton, Longman and Todd, 2007).